The Three Little Pigs

Los Tres Cerditos

Codeswitch castellano english
Texto Bilingüe

Libro 2

Geoff Willis

Copyright © 2023 Geoff Willis

All rights reserved.

No portion of this book, including illustrations, may be reproduced, copied, distributed or adapted in any way, with the exception of certain activities permitted by applicable copyright laws.

Illustrations created by Wafflecaramel, illustrations are the property of Geoff Willis, and subject to copyright.

Reservados todos los derechos

Ninguna parte de este libro, incluidas las ilustraciones, puede reproducirse, copiarse, distribuirse o adaptarse de ninguna manera, con la excepción de ciertas actividades permitidas por las leyes de derechos de autor aplicables.

Ilustraciones creadas por Wafflecaramel, las ilustraciones son propiedad de Geoff Willis y están sujetas a derechos de autor.

Geoff Willis has asserted his right under the Copyright, Designs and Patents Act, 1988, to be identified as the author of this work.

ISBN: 978-1-916738-01-0

This book is for DWS

Thank you for the joy you bring me every day

Ilustración de portada y frontispicio de Wafflecaramel

ÍNDICE

A Introducción   1

B Los Tres Cerditos - Castellano   7

C The Three Little Pigs – Spanish to English   17

D Notas Finales   70

E Un poco de gramática – Verbos estándar   71

F Palabras - Ordenado por Sección   79

G Palabras - Orden Alfabético   91

The Three Little Pigs

A
Introducción

A.1 Objetivo

Este libro es el segundo de una serie de libros de lectura en inglés.

Han sido diseñados para mejorar rápidamente tu capacidad de leer en inglés y que puedas leer textos básicos sin necesidad de usar un diccionario o un libro de gramática.

Los libros *Codeswitch* están diseñados para ser leídos en orden. Este libro está pensado para quienes han leído y comprendido, al menos en lo esencial, el libro 1, *Goldilocks and the Three bears*.

Aprender un nuevo idioma es difícil por dos razones. En primer lugar, la gramática del nuevo idioma es diferente a la de tu propio idioma. En segundo lugar, porque necesitas aprender muchas palabras nuevas.

Los libros *Codeswitch* facilitan el aprendizaje del inglés al copiar cómo los niños aprenden sus propios idiomas.

La historia de este libro usa gramática inglesa completa desde la primera oración, pero el vocabulario comienza casi completamente en castellano.

Luego, se introducen unas pocas palabras en inglés a la vez, de modo que estas nuevas palabras puedan entenderse fácilmente en el contexto de las palabras circundantes en castellano.

De esta forma, tanto la gramática como el vocabulario del inglés se pueden aprender de manera intuitiva; absorbido por ósmosis. Para introducir las nuevas palabras lentamente, las historias se repiten varias veces. Esto también permite la repetición de palabras que sólo se usan una vez en la historia.

A.2 Antecedentes

He llamado a estos libros *Codeswitch* Castellano *English* por un tipo de lenguaje común que se encuentra entre los hablantes bilingües. En *Codeswitch*, «*code*» se usa para significar «idioma», y «*switch*» significa cambiar repentinamente. Entonces, un lenguaje *Codeswitch* es aquel en el que las personas intercambian rápidamente dos idiomas diferentes.

Este libro comienza como un lenguaje *Codeswitch*. Comienza con gramática inglesa y palabras en castellano y te permite cambiar lentamente y, con suerte, sin dolor, del castellano al inglés.

A.3 Estructura

La sección B de este libro es una traducción completa al castellano de *Los tres cerditos*. Puedes leerla primero si no recuerdas la historia. También puedes usar esta versión para comparar la gramática inglesa de la sección C con la gramática del castellano.

Para introducir todas las palabras necesarias en inglés, unas pocas a la vez, la sección C tiene seis versiones mixtas en castellano/inglés. El nivel C.7, que es el último, está escrito en inglés.

Al final del libro he enumerado todo el vocabulario dos veces. Primero, en el orden en que se introducen las palabras, y después, en el orden alfabético de las palabras en inglés.

Las listas de palabras no pretenden ser diccionarios adecuados. Normalmente sólo coloco una traducción simple al castellano. A veces, he intentado capturar palabras con alternativas comunes, especialmente cuando se usa un significado secundario en la historia.

Lo más importante que debes recordar al leer este libro es que todas las historias, desde la primera palabra de la sección C.1, están escritas en gramática inglesa. Esto es cierto y especialmente confuso con el nivel C.1 de este libro, donde muchas de las palabras son en castellano.

A.4 Cómo usar este libro

Cada una de las historias contadas en estos libros se divide en secciones de aproximadamente doscientas palabras cada una.

En cada sección se introduce un promedio de unas cinco palabras nuevas en inglés. El número real de palabras varía, a veces se introducen hasta doce palabras, pero otras veces no se introduce ninguna palabra nueva.

La mejor manera de leer estos libros es mantener la lectura a un nivel cómodo y agradable, repitiendo la lectura.

Entonces, comienza desde el principio y empieza a leer el nivel C.1.01 de este libro. Mientras puedas entender fácilmente la historia, continúa leyendo.

Sigue leyendo hasta que haya demasiadas palabras nuevas y tengas dificultades para comprender lo que sucede en la historia.

Tan pronto como se torne un poco difícil, vuelve a un nivel más fácil.

Te recomiendo retroceder mucho, al menos seis tramos, aunque lo ideal sería retroceder uno o dos niveles. De modo que, si estás a la mitad del nivel C.3 y las cosas se ponen difíciles, regresa al comienzo del nivel C.2 de ese libro.

Si te resulta difícil leer este libro y estás tratando de solucionar las cosas, entonces ya no estás aprendiendo inglés como lo hace un niño.

En este punto, es mejor volver a un lugar del libro donde la lectura sea muy fácil y seguir adelante. Cada vez que hagas esto, verás que avanzas más antes de que el libro se vuelva difícil nuevamente.

A.5 Un poco de gramática

En comparación con la mayoría de los idiomas, el inglés tiene una gramática muy simple, generalmente más simple que la del castellano.

Además, la gramática del inglés y la del castellano son muy similares.

He incluido un poco de gramática en la sección E de cada uno de estos libros. Sin embargo, esto se limita principalmente a áreas donde el inglés es significativamente diferente al castellano.

El libro 1 trata de los sustantivos, en este libro hablaremos de los verbos estándar, el libro 3 de los verbos auxiliares, mientras que el libro 4 analiza los verbos compuestos.

Estas secciones de gramática no son esenciales, si lo prefieres puedes pasar directamente al libro 3 después de leer la sección D.

A.5.1 Palabras confusas

Las palabras de la tabla A.5.1 a continuación tienen la misma ortografía en castellano y en inglés, pero tienen significados diferentes.

En este libro sólo se usan las versiones en inglés, nunca se usan las del castellano.

Tabla A.5.1			
Palabra en los libros	**Pronunciación inglesa**	**En las historias, significa**	**En las historias, nunca significa**
a	a /ə/	un, uno, una	en una dirección
alas	alás /əlás/	¡ay! ¡caramba!	extremidad de un pájaro
come	cum /kəm/	venga, viene	consumir comida
has	has (con «h» no silente)	tiene / ha	segunda persona presente de hacer
he	hii (con «h» no silente)	él	primera persona presente de hacer
once	hü-uns (con «h» silente)	una vez	11
pan	pan	sartén	un bocadillo
use	ius	presente de usar	subjuntivo de usar
vine	vain	vid, planta trepadora, planta enredadera	Pretérito perfecto de venir

Para reducir la confusión, en los libros 1 y 2, en los que hay muchas palabras en castellano, estas se muestran en cursiva.

A.5.2 Palabras con apóstrofos

Las palabras en inglés a veces tienen apóstrofos.

En ocasiones, esto se debe a que las palabras están contraídas, y otras a que son posesivas.

Todos los ejemplos del uso del apóstrofo introducido en este libro se muestran en la tabla A.7.2 a continuación:

Tabla A.5.2		
Contracción	**Forma completa**	**Significado en este libro**
o'clock	*of the clock*	en punto (de hora)
couldn't	*could not*	no podía
didn't	*did not*	no hecho - auxiliar 3.E.3.4.3
don't	*do not*	no hace - auxiliar 3.E.3.4.3
I'll	*I will*	voy a - tiempo futuro 3.E.1
I'm	*I am*	estoy
pig's	posesivo 1.E.3	del cerdo
squire's	posesivo 1.E.3	del hacendado

B

Los Tres Cerditos - Castellano

B.01

Una madre cerdo y sus tres cerditos vivíaron felices juntos en un bosque durante un largo verano. Pero a medida que se acercaba el otoño, la madre cerda llamó a sus pequeños y les dijo;

"Cerditos, ha llegado el momento de que salgan al mundo y busquen su propia fortuna. Cada uno de ustedes necesitará construir una casita para vivir, pero no la construyan con paja o palos; las pajitas son quebradizas y los palitos frágiles.

Construyan sus casas de ladrillos, y siempre tendrán un lugar seguro para vivir; pueden entrar y cerrar la puerta, y nada podia hacerles daño ".

Luego se despidió de los cerditos y estos se fueron al mundo, a hacer fortuna.

El primer cerdito no había ido muy lejos cuando se encontró con un hombre con una carga de paja. La paja parecía tan cálida y olía tan bien que el cerdito olvidó por completo lo que le había dicho su madre.

The Three Little Pigs

"Por favor, señor", dijo el cerdito, "deme suficiente paja para construir una casa y mantenerme caliente durante el largo invierno".

El hombre le dio al cerdito toda la paja que quería y luego se marchó.

B.02

El cerdito se construyó una casa de paja, y era tan cálida y acogedora que estaba encantado con ella.

"Cuanto mejor", dijo, "que una casa de ladrillos duros y fríos".

Así que se quedó allí, cómodo y cálido, pero un día el lobo feroz llamó a la puerta.

"¡Cerdito, cerdito, déjame entrar!" gritó.

"No, por el pelo de mi barbilla-barbilla-barbilla", respondió el cerdo.

"Entonces soplaré, soplaré y derribaré tu casa".

El cerdito se rió a carcajadas, porque se sentía muy en su acogedora casa de paja.

"Bueno, entonces resopla, y luego resopla, ¡y derriba mi casa!" gritó.

Bueno, el lobo resopló y resopló, y derribó la casa; porque solo estaba hecha de paja, y luego se comió el cerdo.

El segundo cerdito salió del bosque y corrió y corrió, hasta que al cabo de un rato se encontró con un hombre con una gran carga de palos.

"Oh, amable señor, por favor deme unos palos para construirme una casita para el invierno", gritó el cerdito.

El hombre estaba feliz de hacer esto. Le dio al cerdo todos los palos que quería y luego siguió su camino.

B.03

El cerdo se construyó una casa de palos que era más fuerte que la casa de paja.

"Qué tonta era mi madre", dijo el cerdo, "al decirme que construyera una casa de ladrillos. ¿Qué podría ser más cálido, acogedor y seguro que esto? "

Y se acurrucó entre las ramas y las hojas y estaba muy feliz.

Poco tiempo después llegó el lobo feroz, se detuvo y llamó a la puerta.

"¡Cerdito, cerdito, déjame entrar!" gritó.

"¡No, por el pelo de mi barbilla-barbilla-barbilla!"

"Entonces soplaré, soplaré y volaré tu casa".

El cerdito se rió al oír eso, porque las paredes eran gruesas y se sintió seguro.

"Bueno, entonces resopla, luego resopla, y derriba mi casa".

Entonces el lobo resopló y resopló, y derribó la casa y se comió el cerdito que estaba dentro.

Ahora el tercer cerdito que era el cerdito más pequeño de todos, pero él era un cerdito muy sabio y decidió hacer exactamente lo que su madre le había dicho que hiciera.

B.04

The Three Little Pigs

Después de salir del bosque, se encontró con el hombre que conducía el carro lleno de paja, pero no le pidió nada.

Luego se encontró con el hombre con la carga de palos, pero no le pidió ninguno de ellos.

Finalmente, se encontró con un hombre con una carga de ladrillos, y solo entonces se detuvo. Pidió tan amablemente ladrillos suficientes para construirse una casita que el hombre no pudo rechazarlo.

El cerdo tomó los ladrillos y se construyó una casita con ellos. Tomó mucho tiempo y mucho trabajo, pero finalmente la casa estaba terminada.

Cuando terminó, no era tan suave como la casita de paja y no estaba tan caliente como la casita de palos, pero era una casita fuerte y muy segura.

Al cabo de un rato llegó el lobo y llamó a la puerta: ¡toc-toc!

"Cerdito, cerdito, déjame entrar", gritó.

"No por el pelo en mi barbilla-barbilla-barbilla".

"Entonces soplaré, soplaré y volaré tu casa".

"Bueno, entonces resopla, luego resopla, y derriba mi casa", respondió el cerdo.

B.05

Así que el lobo resopló y resopló, resopló y resopló, y resopló y resopló hasta que casi se partió los costados, pero no pudo derribar la casa.

Y el cerdito se rió para sí mismo mientras se sentaba seguro y

The Three Little Pigs

cómodo dentro de su casa.

El lobo vio que no había nada que ganar con soplar, así que se sentó y pensó y pensó.

Luego dijo: "Cerdito, sé dónde hay un campo de hermosos nabos".

"¿Dónde?" preguntó el cerdito.

"Abre la puerta y te lo diré".

No, el cerdito podía oír bastante bien con la puerta cerrada.

"Está justo arriba de la carretera, a tres campos de distancia", dijo el lobo, "y si quieres tener un poco, vendré a buscarte a las seis en punto, mañana por la mañana, e iremos a desenterrarlos juntos".

"¡A las seis!" dijo el cerdito. "Muy bien."

Entonces el lobo se fue trotando a casa, lamiendo sus labios. Estaba muy feliz, porque estaba ansioso por desayunar tocino al día siguiente.

Pero a la mañana siguiente, el cerdito estaba levantado y listo a las cinco.

B.06

Trotó hacia el campo de nabos y recogió una bolsa llena de nabos y estuvo de nuevo en casa antes de que llegara el lobo.

A las seis en punto el lobo llamó a la puerta.

"¿Estás listo para ir por los nabos, cerdito?" gritó.

"¡Listo!" respondió el cerdo. "Por qué me levanté y me fui al campo hace una hora y tengo todos los nabos que quiero, y los estoy hirviendo para el desayuno".

The Three Little Pigs

"¿Eso es lo que hiciste?" dijo el lobo. Y luego pensó un poco.

"Cerdito, ¿te gustan las manzanas maduras y jugosas?" preguntó.

Sí, al cerdo le gustaban mucho las manzanas.

"Entonces puedo decirte dónde encontrar algunos".

"¿Donde es eso?"

Más allá de la colina, en el huerto del hacendado, y si no haces ninguna broma, vendré a buscarte mañana a las cinco e iremos juntos a recoger algunas.

Muy bien; el cerdo dijo que estaría listo.

Entonces, el lobo se fue trotando a casa, y esta vez estaba muy seguro de que desayunaría un lindo cerdito gordo a la mañana siguiente.

B.07

El cerdito se levantó a las cuatro en punto del día siguiente y se fue al huerto tan rápido como sus cuatro patitas lo permitían.

Pero el camino era largo y era difícil trepar por el árbol, y mientras él todavía estaba entre las ramas recogiendo manzanas, el lobo feroz entró corriendo en el huerto.

El cerdito estaba muy asustado, pero se quedó muy quieto y esperaba, entre las hojas, que el lobo no lo viera.

El lobo miró a su alrededor, primero subió a un árbol y luego a otro, y finalmente vio al cerdo entre las ramas.

"¿Por qué no me esperaste?"

"Oh, sabía que llegarías pronto".

"¿Qué tan pronto vas a bajar?"

"Cuando haya recogido algunas manzanas más".

El lobo se sentó al pie del árbol y el cerdo se sentó entre las ramas, masticando manzanas y lamiéndose los labios.

"¿Están bien?" preguntó el lobo mirando hacia arriba; se le hacía agua la boca.

Sí, estaban muy buenas.

"Por favor, ¿podrías arrojarme uno?"

Sí, el cerdito podría hacer eso.

B.08

Cogió la manzana más grande y roja que pudo, y luego la tiró, pero la tiró lo más lejos que pudo, y de tal manera que fue rebotando y rodando por la ladera del cerro.

El lobo saltó colina abajo tras ella, y mientras la atrapaba, el cerdito bajó del árbol y corrió sano y salvo a casa con su canasta llena de manzanas.

Cuando el lobo descubrió que el cerdo lo había engañado nuevamente, se enojó mucho. Estaba más decidido que nunca a atrapar al cerdito.

Trotó hasta la casita y llamó a la puerta.

"¿Conseguiste todas las manzanas que querías?" preguntó el lobo.

Sí, el cerdito tenía todo lo que quería y le agradeció al lobo por contarle sobre el huerto.

"Escucha, cerdito, mañana habrá una hermosa feria en la ciudad", dijo el lobo.

The Three Little Pigs

"¿Te gustaría ir?"

Sí, al cerdito le gustaría mucho ir.

"Muy bien", dijo el lobo. "Entonces vendré a buscarte mañana a las tres y media, e iremos juntos".

B.09

"Muy bien," dijo el cerdito. Pero mucho antes de las tres y media del día siguiente, el cerdito se fue a la feria y se llevó cuatro monedas de plata brillante, porque quería comprarse una mantequera.

No tardó en comprar la lechera y luego volvió a casa, cargándola a la espalda.

Pero el lobo había aprendido un par de cosas sobre los trucos del cerdito.

Él también partió hacia la feria mucho antes de las tres y media, de modo que el cerdito estaba a medio camino de su casa y acababa de llegar a la cima de una colina alta, cuando vio que el lobo subía a grandes zancadas. colina directamente hacia él.

El cerdito estaba aterrorizado. Miró a su alrededor, pero no vio ningún lugar donde esconderse. Decidió que lo mejor que podía hacer era meterse en la lechera.

Así que lo dejó y se arrastró dentro. Pero la colina era muy empinada, y tan pronto como el cerdo estuvo dentro de la lechera, comenzó a rodar por la ladera de la colina, golpe, golpe, golpe, sobre rocas y piedras, saltando y rebotando como algo vivo.

B.10

El cerdito no sabía lo que le estaba pasando. Comenzó a chillar a todo pulmón.

El lobo estaba a la mitad de la colina cuando escuchó el ruido. Miró hacia arriba, y había una gran cosa redonda que se acercaba rebotando sobre las rocas directamente hacia él, chillando y chillando mientras se acercaba.

Lanzó una mirada y su cabello se erizó por el miedo, y con un aullido se dio la vuelta y corrió a casa lo más rápido que pudo.

No se detuvo hasta que estuvo a salvo dentro de su casa, y había cerrado y bloqueado la puerta detrás de él.

Allí se agachó, temblando y preguntándose qué pasaría.

Pero no pasó nada y todo estaba en silencio, así que después de un rato el lobo salió y corrió hacia la casa del cerdo.

"¡Cerdito, cerdito! ¿Estas ahi?"

Sí, el cerdito estaba sentado junto al fuego asando manzanas.

"Entonces escucha mientras te cuento lo que me pasó camino a la feria".

Entonces el lobo acercó la nariz a la rendija de la puerta y le contó al cerdito todo sobre la gran cosa redonda y chillona que lo había perseguido colina abajo.

B.11

El cerdito se rió y rió.

"Puedo decirte exactamente cuál fue el gran chillido; era una lechera que compré en la feria, y yo estaba dentro ".

Cuando el lobo escuchó esto, se enojó tanto que decidió quedarse con el cerdito, aunque tuviera que trepar al techo y bajar por la chimenea a buscarlo.

Metió sus afiladas garras entre los ladrillos de la casa y trepó por un costado hasta el techo.

Luego se subió a la chimenea y se deslizó por la chimenea.

Pero el cerdito había escuchado lo que estaba haciendo y estaba listo para él.

Tenía una olla grande con agua hirviendo en el fuego, y cuando escuchó al lobo deslizarse y gatear por la chimenea, quitó la tapa de la olla y PLAF... el lobo cayó directamente al agua hirviendo.

Entonces el cerdito puso la tapa hermética sobre la olla, y ese fue el final del lobo feroz.

El cerdito vivió en paz y en abundancia para siempre, y si algún otro lobo llegó a molestarlo, yo nunca supe de eso.

C

The Three Little Pigs - Spanish to English

Tenga en cuenta que los niveles C.1 y C.2 son más cortos con un vocabulario reducido. Esto es para permitir que se introduzcan nuevas palabras, unas cuantas a la vez.

The Three Little *Cerdos*

C.1.01

A mother *cerdo* and her three little *cerdos vivían juntos felizmente* in a *bosque*. One day the mother *cerdo* said;

"Little *cerdos*, the time has come for you to *ir* out and *buscar* your *fortunas*. You will *necesitar* to *construir* a little house to *vivir* in, but do not *construir* them of *paja o palos*.

Construid your houses of *ladrillos*, then you will have a *seguro sitio* to *vivir* in.

The first little *cerdo completamente olvidó* what his mother had *dicho* him.

The little *cerdo construyó* himself a house of *paja*, and it was so *tibia* and *acogedora* that he was *encantado* with it.

The Three Little Pigs

"How *mucho mejor*," he said "than a house of cold hard *ladrillos*."

So he lay there *acogedor* and *tibio*, but one day the big *malo lobo* knocked on the door.

"Little *cerdo*, little *cerdo*, let me in!" he cried.

"No" answered the *cerdo*.

"Then *yo* will *soplar*, and *yo* will *resoplar*, and *yo* will *soplar* your house down."

The little *cerdo rio* out *ruidoso*, for he felt very *seguro* in his *acogedora paja* house.

"Then *sopla*, and then *resopla*, and *sopla* my house down!" he cried.

The *lobo* did *soplar* and *resoplar*, and he did *soplar* the house down, and then he ate the *cerdo* up.

C.1.02

The second little *cerdo construyó* himself a house of *palos* and it was stronger than the *paja* house.

"How *tonta* my mother was," said the *cerdo*, "to *decir* me to *construir* a *ladrillo* house. What could be *más tibio* and *acogedor* and *seguro* than this?"

And he *acurrucó* down *entre* the *ramas* and *hojas* and was very *feliz*.

A little time *mas tarde* the big *malo lobo* came, and he stopped and knocked on the door.

"Little *cerdo*, little *cerdo*, let me in!" he cried.

"No" answered the *cerdo*.

"Then I will *soplar*, and I will *resoplar*, and I will *soplar* your house down."

The little *cerdo rio* when he heard that, for the *paredes* were *gruesas*, and he felt *seguro*.

"Then *sopla*, and then *resopla*, and *sopla* my house down."

So the *lobo sopló*, and he *resopló*, and he did *soplar* the house down, and he ate up the little *cerdo* that was inside.

C.1.03

Now the third little *cerdo* was the smallest *cerdo* of all, but he was a very *sabio* little *cerdo*, and he *decidió* to do *exactamente* what his mother had *dicho* him to do.

The *cerdo construyó* himself a little house of *ladrillos*.

When it was done it was not as soft as the little *paja* house, and it was not as *tibio* as the little *palo* house, but it was a very *segura* strong little house.

After a time the *lobo* came and knocked on the door.

"Little *cerdo*, little *cerdo*, let me in," he called.

"No" answered the *cerdo*.

"Then I will *soplar*, and I will *resoplar*, and I will *soplar* your house down."

"Then *sopla*, and then *resopla*, and *sopla* my house down," answered the *cerdo*.

So the *lobo sopló* and he *resopló*, and he *resopló* and he *sopló*, and he *SOPLÓ* AND HE *RESOPLÓ* until he *casi separó* his *lados*, but he could not *soplar* the house down.

The Three Little Pigs

And the little *cerdo rio* to himself as he sat *seguro* and comfortable inside his house.

C.1.04

When the *lobo* heard this, he was so *enfadado* that he *decidió* to have the little *cerdo, incluso* if he had to *trepar* up on the *techo* and *ir* down the *chimenea*.

He *metió* his sharp *garras* in *entre* the *ladrillos* of the house and *trepó* right up the *lado* of it and onto the *techo*.

Then he *trepó* up on to the *chimenea* and *resbaló* down inside it.

But the little *cerdo* had heard what he was doing, and was *listo* for him.

He had a big *olla* of *hirviendo agua* on the *fuego*, and when he heard the *lobo resbalando* and *escarbando* down the *chimenea*, and *plaf…* the *lobo* fell right in the *hirviendo agua*.

Then the little *cerdo puso* the *tapa* tight down onto the *olla*, and that was the end of the big *malo lobo*.

The little *cerdo vivió* on in *paz* and *abundancia* forever after, and if *algún otro lobo* ever came along to *molestar* him, I never heard about it.

The Three Little Pigs

C.2.01

A mother pig and her three little pigs *vivían juntos felizmente* in a *bosque*. One day the mother pig said;

"Little pigs, the time has come for you to *ir* out and seek your *fortunas*. Each of you will *necesitar* to *construir* a little house to *vivir* in, but do not *construir* them of *paja* o *palos*.

Construid your houses of *ladrillos*, then you will have a *seguro sitio* to *vivir* in.

The first little pig *completamente olvidó* what his mother had *dicho* him.

The little pig *construyó* himself a house of *paja*, and it was so *tibia* and *acogedora* that he was *encantado* with it.

"How *mucho* better," he said "than a house of cold hard *ladrillos*."

So he lay there *acogedor* and warm, but one day the big *malo* wolf knocked on the door.

"Little pig, little pig, let me in!" he cried.

"No" answered the pig.

"Then I will *soplar*, and I will *resoplar*, and I will *soplar* your house down."

The little pig *rio* out *ruidoso*, for he felt very *seguro* in his *acogedora paja* house.

"Then *sopla*, and then *resopla*, and *sopla* my house down!" he cried.

The wolf did *soplar* and *resoplar*, and he did *soplar* the house down, and then he ate the pig up.

The Three Little Pigs

C.2.02

The second little pig *construyó* himself a house of *palos* and it was stronger than the *paja* house.

"How *tonta* my mother was," said the pig, "to *decir* me to *construir* a *ladrillo* house. What could be *más* warm and *acogedor* and *seguro* than this?"

And he *acurrucó* down *entre* the *ramas* and *hojas* and was very *feliz*.

A little time later the big *malo* wolf came, and he stopped and knocked on the door.

"Little pig, little pig, let me in!" he cried.

"No" answered the pig.

"Then I will *soplar*, and I will *resoplar*, and I will blow your house down."

The little pig *rio* when he heard that, for the *paredes* were *grueso*, and he felt *seguro*.

"Then *sopla*, and then *resopla*, and blow my house down."

So the wolf *sopló*, and he *resopló*, and he did blow the house down, and he ate up the little pig that was inside.

C.2.03

Now the third little pig was the smallest pig of all, but he was a very wise little pig, and he *decidió* to do *exactamente* what his mother had *dicho* him to do.

The pig *construyó* himself a little house of *ladrillos*.

The Three Little Pigs

When it was done it was not as soft as the little *paja* house, and it was not as warm as the little *palo* house, but it was a very *segura* strong little house.

After a time the wolf came and knocked on the door – knock-knock!

"Little pig, little pig, let me in," he called.

"No" answered the pig.

"Then I will *soplar*, and I will *resoplar*, and I will blow your house down."

"Then *sopla*, and then *resopla*, and blow my house down," answered the pig.

So the wolf *sopló* and he *resopló*, and he *resopló* and he *sopló*, and he SOPLÓ AND HE RESOPLÓ till he *casi separó* his sides, but he couldn't blow the house down.

And the little pig *rio* to himself as he sat *seguro* and comfortable inside his house.

C.2.04

When the wolf heard this, he was so *enfadado* that he *decidió* to have the little pig, even if he had to *trepar* up on the *techo* and *ir* down the chimney.

He *metió* his sharp claws in *entre* the *ladrillos* of the house and *trepó* right up the side of it and onto the *techo*.

Then he *trepó* up on to the chimney and *resbaló* down inside it.

But the little pig had heard what he was doing, and was *listo* for him.

He had a big *olla* of *hirviendo agua* on the *fuego*, and when he heard the wolf slipping and scrabbling down the chimney, and *plaf*... the wolf fell right in the *hirviendo agua*.

Then the little pig *puso* the *tapa* tight down onto the *olla*, and that was the end of the big *malo* wolf.

The little pig *vivió* on in *paz* and *abundancia* forever after, and if any other wolf ever came along to bother him, I never heard about it.

The Three Little Pigs

C.3.01

A mother pig and her three little pigs *vivían juntos felizmente* in a wood all through a *largo verano*. But as *otoño acercó* the mother pig called her little ones to her and said;

"Little pigs, the time has come for you to *ir* out into the *mundo* and seek your *propias fortunas*. Each of you will *necesitar* to *construir* a little house to *vivir* in, but do not *construir* them of *paja o palos; pajas* are *frágil* and *palos* are *débil*.

Construid your houses of *ladrillos*, then you will always have a *seguro sitio* to *vivir* in; you can *ir* in and lock the door, and *nada* can *dañar* you."

Then she said *adiós* to the little pigs, and *fuera* they went, out into the *mundo*, to make their *fortunas*.

The first little pig had not gone *lejos* when he *encontró* an hombre with a *carga* of *paja*. The *paja* looked so *tibia*, and smelled so good that the little pig *completamente olvidó* what his mother had *dicho* him.

"*Por favor, señor,*" said the little pig, "give me *suficiente paja* to *construir* a house to *guardar* me warm through the *largo invierno*."

The *hombre* gave the little pig all the *paja* he wanted, and then he *condujo fuera*.

C.3.02

The little pig *construyó* himself a house of *paja,* and it was so *tibia* and *acogedora* that he was *encantado* with it.

"How *mucho* better," he said "than a house of cold hard *ladrillos.*"

So he lay there *acogedor* and warm, but one day the big *malo* wolf knocked on the door.

"Little pig, little pig, let me in!" he cried.

"Not by the hair on my chinny-chin-chin," answered the pig.

"Then I'll *soplar,* and I'll *resoplar,* and I'll blow your house down."

The little pig *rio* out *ruidoso,* for he felt very *seguro* in his *acogedora paja* house.

"Well, then *sopla,* and then *resopla,* and blow my house down!" he cried.

Well, the wolf did *soplar* and *resoplar,* and he did blow the house down; because it was *solamente* made of *paja,* and then he ate the pig up.

The second little pig left the forest and ran and ran, until after a time he *encontró* an *hombre* with a big *carga* of *palos.*

"Oh, amable *señor, por favor* give me some *palos* to *construir* me a little house for the *invierno* time," cried the little pig.

The *hombre* was *feliz* to do this. He gave the pig all the *palos* he wanted, and then he went on his way.

The Three Little Pigs

C.3.03

The pig *construyó* himself a house of *palos* and it was stronger than the *paja* house had been.

"How *tonta* my mother was," said the pig, "to *decir* me to *construir* a *ladrillo* house. What could be *más* warm and *acogedor* and *seguro* than this?"

And he *acurrucó* down *entre* the *ramas* and *hojas* and was very *feliz*.

A little time later along came the big *malo* wolf, and he stopped and knocked on the door.

"Little pig, little pig, let me in!" he cried.

"Not by the hair of my chinny-chin-chin!"

"Then I'll *soplar*, and I'll *resoplar*, and I'll blow your house down."

The little pig *rio* when he heard that, for the *paredes* were *grueso*, and he felt *seguro*.

"Well, then *sopla*, and then *resopla*, and blow my house down."

So the wolf *sopló*, and he *resopló*, and he did blow the house down, and he ate up the little pig that was inside.

Now the third little pig was the smallest pig of all, but he was a very wise little pig, and he *decidió* to do *exactamente* what his mother had *dicho* him to do.

C.3.04

After he left the forest, he *encontró* the *hombre conduciendo* the *vagón* full of *paja*, but he did not *preguntar* for *algo* of it.

Then he *encontró* the *hombre* with the *carga* of *palos*, but he did

The Three Little Pigs

not *preguntar* for *algo* of them.

Finally, he *encontró* an *hombre* with a *carga* of *ladrillos*, and *solamente* then did he stop. He *preguntó* so nicely for *suficiente ladrillos* to *construir* himself a little house that the *hombre* could not *rehusar* him.

The pig took the *ladrillos* and *construyó* himself a little house with them. It took a lot of time and a lot of *trabajo*, but finally the house was *terminada*.

When it was done it was not as soft as the little *paja* house, and it was not as warm as the little *palo* house, but it was a very *segura* strong little house.

After a time the wolf came along and knocked on the door – knock-knock!

"Little pig, little pig, let me in," he called.

"Not by the hair on my chinny-chin-chin."

"Then I'll *soplar*, and I'll *resoplar*, and I'll blow your house down."

"Well, then *sopla*, and then *resopla*, and blow my house down," answered the pig.

C.3.05

So the wolf *sopló* and he *resopló*, and he *resopló* and he *sopló*, and he *SOPLÓ* AND HE *RESOPLÓ* till he *casi separó* his sides, but he couldn't blow the house down.

And the little pig *rio* to himself as he sat *seguro* and comfortable inside his house.

The wolf *vio* there was *nada* to *ganar* by blowing, so he sat down and thought and thought.

The Three Little Pigs

Then he said, "Little pig, I know *donde* there is a *campo* of fine *nabos*."

"*Donde*?" *preguntó* the little pig.

"Open the door and I will *decir* you."

No, the little pig could hear *bastante* well with the door *cerrado*.

"It is just up the road three *campos fuera*," said the wolf, "and if you would like to have some, I will come for you at *seis* o'clock tomorrow morning, and *nosotros* will *ir* and *cavar* them up *juntos*."

"At *seis* o'clock!" said the little pig. "Very good."

Then the wolf *trotó* off home, *lamiendo* his *labios*. He was very *feliz*, because he was looking forward to having *tocino* for breakfast the *próximo* day.

But the *próximo* morning the little pig was up and *listo* by *cinco* o'clock.

C.3.06

Off he *trotó* to the *nabo campo* and gathered an *entero bolsa* full of *nabos* and was home again before the wolf *llegó*.

At *seis* o'clock the wolf knocked on the door.

"Are you *listo* to ir for the *nabos*, little pig?" he cried.

"*Listo!*" answered the pig. "Why, I was up and off to the *campo* an *hora* ago and I have all the *nabos* I want, and I'm *hirviendo* them for breakfast."

"Is that what you did?" said the wolf. And then he thought for a bit.

"Little pig, do you like *maduras jugosas manzanas*?" he *preguntó*.

Sí, the pig was very fond of *manzanas*.

The Three Little Pigs

"Then I can *decir* you *donde* to *encontrar* some."

"*Donde* is that?"

"Over beyond the *colina* in the squire's *huerta*, and if you don't play *algún truco* I will come for you at *cinco* o'clock tomorrow, and *nosotros* will *ir juntos*, and gather some."

Very well; the pig said he would be *listo*.

So, the wolf *trotó* off home, and this time he was very *seguro* that he would have a nice *gordo* little pig for breakfast the *próximo* morning.

C.3.07

The little pig got up at *cuatro* o'clock the *próximo* day, and off he went to the *huerta* as fast as his *cuatro* little feet would *llevar* him.

But the way was *largo*, and the tree was hard to *trepar*, and while he was still up *entre* the *ramas* gathering *manzanas* the big *malo* wolf came *dando zancadas* into the *huerta*.

The little pig was very *aterrado*, but he *guardó* very *calma* and hoped, up *entre* the *hojas*, the wolf would not see him.

The wolf peered around, first up one tree and then up another, and finally he *divisó* the pig up *entre* the *ramas*.

"Why didn't you wait for me?"

"Oh, I knew you would be along soon."

"How soon are you coming down?"

"When I have picked a *poco más manzanas*."

The wolf sat down at the foot of the tree, and the pig sat up entre the *ramas crujiendo manzanas* and *lamiendo* his *labios*.

The Three Little Pigs

"Are they good?" *preguntó* the wolf looking up.

Sí, they were very good.

"*Por favor* could you *lanzar* one down to me?"

Sí, the little pig could do that.

C.3.08

He picked the biggest, reddest *manzana* he could, and then he *lanzó* it, but he *lanzó* it as *lejos* as he could, and in such a way that it went *rebotando* and rolling down the *cuesta* of the *colina*.

The wolf *brincó* down the *colina* after it, and while he was *capturando* it, the little pig *trepó* down the tree and ran *seguramente* home with his basketful of *manzanas*.

When the wolf *encontró* the pig had *engañado* him again, he was very *enfadado*. He was *más determinado* than ever that he would *capturar* the little pig.

He *trotó* off to the little house and knocked on the door.

"Did you get all the *manzanas* you wanted?" *preguntó* the wolf.

Sí, the little pig had all he wanted, and he *agradeció* the wolf for *diciendo* him about the *huerta*.

"*Escucha*, little pig, there will be a fine *feria* over in the *pueblo* tomorrow," said the wolf.

"Would you like to go?"

Sí, the little pig would very *mucho* like to go.

"Very well," said the wolf. "Then I will come for you at half-past three tomorrow, and *nosotros* will ir *juntos*."

The Three Little Pigs

C.3.09

"Very well," said the little pig. But *largo* before half-past three the *próximo* day, little pig went off to the *feria*, and he took *cuatro* bright silver *monedas* with him, because he wanted to *comprar* himself a *mantequilla* lechera.

It did not take him *largo* to *comprar* the *lechera*, and then he *empezó* home again, *llevando* it on his back.

But the wolf had *aprendido* a *cosa o dos* about the little pig's *trucos*.

He, too, *empezó* off to the *feria largo* before half-past three, and so it was that the little pig was *solamente* half way home, and had just reached the *cima* of a high *colina*, when he *vio* the wolf come *dando zancadas* up the *colina directamente hacia* him.

The little pig was *aterrorizado*. He looked all around but he couldn't see *algún sitio* to *esconder*. He *decidió* the best *cosa* he could do was to get inside the *lechera*.

So he *puso* it down and *trepó* inside it. But the *colina* was very *empinado*, and no sooner was the pig inside the *lechera* than it *empezó* to roll down the *colina cuesta* - *choca, choca, choca* - over *rocas* and *piedras*, leaping and *rebotando* like *algo vivo*.

C.3.10

The little pig did not know what was *sucediendo* to him. He *empezó* to squeal at the *cima* of his voice.

The wolf was half-way up the *colina* when he heard the *ruido*. He looked up, and there was a great *redonda cosa* coming *rebotando* over the *rocas directo* at him, squeaking and squealing as it came.

He gave one look and his hair *erizó* with *miedo*, and with an *aullido* he *giró redondo* and ran home as fast as he could.

The Three Little Pigs

He didn't stop till he was *seguro* inside his house, and had *cerrado* and locked the door *detrás* him.

There he *agachó, temblando* and wondering what would *suceder*.

But *nada sucedió*, and everything was *tranquilo*, so after a time the wolf went out and ran over to the pig's house.

"Little pig, little pig! Are you in there?"

Sí, the little pig was sitting by the fire *asando manzanas*.

"Then, *escucha* while I *digo* you what *sucedió* to me on the way to the *feria*."

Then the wolf *puso* his *nariz cerca* to the *grieta* of the door, and *dijo* the little pig all about the great *redonda* squealing *cosa* that had *perseguido* him down the *colina*.

C.3.11

The little pig *rio* and *rio*.

"I can *decir* you *exactamente* what the great squealing *cosa* was; it was a *lechera* which I *compró* at the *feria*, and I was inside it."

When the wolf heard this, he was so *enfadado* that he *decidió* to have the little pig, even if he had to *trepar* up on the *techo* and *ir* down the chimney to get him.

He *metió* his sharp claws in *entre* the *ladrillos* of the house and *trepó* right up the side of it and onto the *techo*.

Then he *trepó* up on to the chimney and *resbaló* down it, into the fireplace.

But the little pig had heard what he was doing, and was *listo* for him.

He had a big *olla* of *hirviendo agua* on the fire, and when he heard the wolf slipping and scrabbling down the chimney, he took the *tapa* off the *olla*, and *plaf*... the wolf fell right into the *hirviendo agua*.

Then the little pig *puso* the *tapa* tight down onto the *olla*, and that was the end of the big *malo* wolf.

The little pig *vivió* on in *paz* and *abundancia* forever after, and if *algún* other wolf ever came along to bother him, I never heard about it.

The Three Little Pigs

C.4.01

A mother pig and her three little pigs *vivían juntos felizmente* in a wood all through a *largo* summer. But as autumn approached the mother pig called her little ones to her and said;

"Little pigs, the time has come for you to *ir* out into the *mundo* and seek your *propias fortunas*. Each of you will *necesitar* to *construir* a little house to *vivir* in, but do not *construir* them of *paja* o *palos; pajas* are brittle and *palos* are frail.

Construid your houses of *ladrillos*, then you will always have a *seguro sitio* to *vivir* in; you can *ir* in and lock the door, and *nada* can *dañar* you."

Then she said goodbye to the little pigs, and away they went, out into the *mundo*, to make their *fortunas*.

The first little pig had not gone *lejos* when he *encontró* an *hombre* with a *carga* of *paja*. The *paja* looked so *tibia*, and smelled so good that the little pig *completamente olvidó* what his mother had *dicho* him.

The Three Little Pigs

"*Por favor*, sir," said the little pig, "give me *suficiente paja* to *construir* a house to *guardar* me warm through the *largo invierno*."

The *hombre* gave the little pig all the *paja* he wanted, and then he *condujo* away.

C.4.02

The little pig *construyó* himself a house of *paja*, and it was so warm and cosy that he was *encantado* with it.

"How *mucho* better," he said "than a house of cold hard *ladrillos*."

So he lay there *acogedor* and warm, but one day the big *malo* wolf knocked on the door.

"Little pig, little pig, let me in!" he cried.

"Not by the hair on my chinny-chin-chin," answered the pig.

"Then I'll *soplar*, and I'll *resoplar*, and I'll blow your house down."

The little pig *rio* out loud, for he felt very *seguro* in his *acogedora paja* house.

"Well, then *sopla*, and then *resopla*, and blow my house down!" he cried.

Well, the wolf did *soplar* and *resoplar*, and he did blow the house down; because it was *solamente* made of *paja*, and then he ate the pig up.

The second little pig left the forest and ran and ran, until after a time he *encontró* an *hombre* with a big *carga* of *palos*.

"Oh, kind sir, *por favor* give me some *palos* to *construir* me a little house for the *invierno* time," cried the little pig.

The *hombre* was *feliz* to do this. He gave the pig all the *palos* he wanted, and then he went on his way.

C.4.03

The pig *construyó* himself a house of *palos* and it was stronger than the *paja* house had been.

"How silly my mother was," said the pig, "to *decir* me to *construir* a *ladrillo* house. What could be *más* warm and cosy and *seguro* than this?"

And he snuggled down *entre* the *ramas* and *hojas* and was very *feliz*.

A little time later along came the big *malo* wolf, and he stopped and knocked on the door.

"Little pig, little pig, let me in!" he cried.

"Not by the hair of my chinny-chin-chin!"

"Then I'll *soplar*, and I'll *resoplar*, and I'll blow your house down."

The little pig *rio* when he heard that, for the walls were thick, and he felt secure.

"Well, then *sopla*, and then *resopla*, and blow my house down."

So the wolf *sopló*, and he *resopló*, and he did blow the house down, and he ate up the little pig that was inside.

Now the third little pig was the smallest pig of all, but he was a very wise little pig, and he *decidió* to do *exactamente* what his mother had *dicho* him to do.

The Three Little Pigs

C.4.04

After he left the forest, he *encontró* the *hombre conduciendo* the wagon full of *paja*, but he did not *preguntar* for *algo* of it.

Then he *encontró* the *hombre* with the *carga* of *palos*, but he did not *preguntar* for *algo* of them.

Finally, he *encontró* an *hombre* with a *carga* of *ladrillos*, and *solamente* then did he stop. He *preguntó* so nicely for *suficiente ladrillos* to *construir* himself a little house that the *hombre* could not *rehusar* him.

The pig took the *ladrillos* and *construyó* himself a little house with them. It took a lot of time and a lot of *trabajo*, but finally the house was *terminada*.

When it was done it was not as soft as the little *paja* house, and it was not as *tibia* as the little *palo* house, but it was a very *segura* strong little house.

After a time the wolf came along and knocked on the door – knock-knock!

"Little pig, little pig, let me in," he called.

"Not by the hair on my chinny-chin-chin."

"Then I'll *soplar*, and I'll *resoplar*, and I'll blow your house down."

"Well, then *sopla*, and then *resopla*, and blow my house down," answered the pig.

C.4.05

So the wolf *sopló* and he *resopló*, and he *resopló* and he *sopló*, and he *SOPLÓ* AND HE *RESOPLÓ* till he *casi* split his sides, but he couldn't blow the house down.

The Three Little Pigs

And the little pig *rio* to himself as he sat *seguro* and comfortable inside his house.

The wolf *vio* there was *nada* to gain by blowing, so he sat down and thought and thought.

Then he said, "Little pig, I know where there is a *campo* of fine *nabos*."

"Where?" *preguntó* the little pig.

"Open the door and I will *decir* you."

No, the little pig could hear *bastante* well with the door *cerrado*.

"It is just up the road three *campos* away," said the wolf, "and if you would like to have some, I will come for you at *seis* o'clock tomorrow morning, and *nosotros* will *ir* and dig them up *juntos*."

"At *seis* o'clock!" said the little pig. "Very good."

Then the wolf *trotó* off home, *lamiendo* his *labios*. He was very *feliz*, because he was looking forward to having bacon for breakfast the *próximo* day.

But the *próximo* morning the little pig was up and *listo* by *cinco* o'clock.

C.4.06

Off he *trotó* to the *nabo campo* and gathered an *entero bolsa* full of *nabos* and was home again before the wolf arrived.

At *seis* o'clock the wolf knocked on the door.

"Are you *listo* to *ir* for the *nabos*, little pig?" he cried.

The Three Little Pigs

"*Listo!*" answered the pig. "Why, I was up and off to the *campo* an *hora* ago and I have all the *nabos* I want, and I'm *hirviendo* them for breakfast."

"Is that what you did?" said the wolf. And then he thought for a bit.

"Little pig, do you like ripe juicy *manzanas*?" he *preguntó*.

Sí, the pig was very fond of *manzanas*.

"Then I can *decir* you where to *encontrar* some."

"Where is that?"

"Over beyond the *colina* in the squire's *huerta*, and if you don't play *algún truco* I will come for you at *cinco* o'clock tomorrow, and *nosotros* will *ir juntos*, and gather some."

Very well; the pig said he would be *listo*.

So, the wolf *trotó* off home, and this time he was very *seguro* that he would have a nice fat little pig for breakfast the *próximo* morning.

C.4.07

The little pig got up at *cuatro* o'clock the *próximo* day, and off he went to the *huerta* as fast as his *cuatro* little feet would *llevar* him.

But the way was *largo*, and the tree was hard to *trepar*, and while he was still up *entre* the *ramas* gathering *manzanas* the big *malo* wolf came *dando zancadas* into the *huerta*.

The little pig was very *aterrado*, but he *guardó* very *calma* and hoped, up *entre* the *hojas*, the wolf would not see him.

The wolf peered around, first up one tree and then up another, and finally he spotted the pig up *entre* the *ramas*.

"Why didn't you wait for me?"

The Three Little Pigs

"Oh, I knew you would be along soon."

"How soon are you coming down?"

"When I have picked a *poco más manzanas*."

The wolf sat down at the foot of the tree, and the pig sat up *entre* the *ramas* crunching *manzanas* and *lamiendo* his *labios*.

"Are they good?" *preguntó* the wolf looking up; his mouth watering.

Sí, they were very good.

"*Por favor* could you *lanzar* one down to me?"

Sí, the little pig could do that.

C.4.08

He picked the biggest, reddest *manzana* he could, and then he *lanzó* it, but he *lanzó* it as *lejos* as he could, and in such a way that it went *rebotando* and rolling down the *cuesta* of the *colina*.

The wolf bounded down the *colina* after it, and while he was *capturando* it, the little pig *trepó* down the tree and ran *seguramente* home with his basketful of *manzanas*.

When the wolf *encontró* the pig had *engañó* him again, he was very *enfadado*. He was *más* determined than ever that he would *capturar* the little pig.

He *trotó* off to the little house and knocked on the door.

"Did you get all the *manzanas* you wanted?" *preguntó* the wolf.

Sí, the little pig had all he wanted, and he *agradeció* the wolf for *diciendo* him about the *huerta*.

"*Escucha*, little pig, there will be a fine fair over in the town tomorrow," said the wolf.

The Three Little Pigs

"Would you like to go?"

Sí, the little pig would very *mucho* like to go.

"Very well," said the wolf. "Then I will come for you at half-past three tomorrow, and *nosotros* will *ir juntos*."

C.4.09

"Very well," said the little pig. But *largo* before half-past three the *próximo* day, little pig went off to the fair, and he took *cuatro* bright silver *monedas* with him, because he wanted to *comprar* himself a *mantequilla lechera*.

It did not take him *largo* to *comprar* the *lechera*, and then he *empezó* home again, *llevando* it on his back.

But the wolf had *aprendido* a thing *o dos* about the little pig's *trucos*.

He, too, *empezó* off to the fair *largo* before half-past three, and so it was that the little pig was *solamente* half way home, and had just reached the *cima* of a high *colina*, when he *vio* the wolf come *dando zancadas* up the *colina* directly *hacia* him.

The little pig was *aterrorizado*. He looked all around but he couldn't see *algún sitio* to *esconder*. He *decidió* the best thing he could do was to get inside the *lechera*.

So he *puso* it down and *trepó* inside it. But the *colina* was very steep, and no sooner was the pig inside the *lechera* than it *empezó* to roll down the *colina cuesta* - bump, bump, bump - over *rocas* and *piedras*, leaping and *rebotando* like something vivo.

C.4.10

The little pig did not know what was *sucediendo* to him. He *empezó* to squeal at the *cima* of his voice.

The Three Little Pigs

The wolf was half-way up the *colina* when he heard the *ruido*. He looked up, and there was a great round thing coming *rebotando* over the *rocas directo* at him, squeaking and squealing as it came.

He gave one look and his hair bristled with *miedo*, and with an *aullido* he *giró* round and ran home as fast as he could.

He didn't stop till he was *seguro* inside his house, and had *cerrado* and locked the door *detrás* him.

There he crouched, *temblando* and wondering what would *suceder*.

But nothing *sucedió,* and everything was quiet, so after a time the wolf went out and ran over to the pig's house.

"Little pig, little pig! Are you in there?"

Sí, the little pig was sitting by the fire *asando manzanas*.

"Then, *escucha* while I *digo* you what *sucedió* to me on the way to the fair."

Then the wolf *puso* his *nariz cerca* to the *grieta* of the door, and *dijo* the little pig all about the great round squealing thing that had chased him down the *colina*.

C.4.11

The little pig *rio* and *rio*.

"I can *decir* you *exactamente* what the great squealing thing was; it was a *lechera* which I bought at the fair, and I was inside it."

When the wolf heard this, he was so *enfadado* that he *decidió* to have the little pig, even if he had to *trepar* up on the *techo* and *ir* down the chimney to get him.

He stuck his sharp claws in between the *ladrillos* of the house and *trepó* right up the side of it and onto the *techo*.

Then he *trepó* up on to the chimney and slid down it, into the fireplace.

But the little pig had heard what he was doing, and was *listo* for him.

He had a big *olla* of *hirviendo agua* on the fire, and when he heard the wolf slipping and scrabbling down the chimney, he took the *tapa* off the *olla*, and *plaf*... the wolf fell right into the *hirviendo agua*.

Then the little pig *puso* the *tapa* tight down onto the *olla*, and that was the end of the big *malo* wolf.

The little pig *vivió* on in *paz* and *abundancia* forever after, and if *algún* other wolf ever came along to bother him, I never heard about it.

The Three Little Pigs

C.5.01

A mother pig and her three little pigs *vivían juntos* happily in a wood all through a *largo* summer. But as autumn approached the mother pig called her little ones to her and said;

"Little pigs, the time has come for you to *ir* out into the *mundo* and seek your *propias* fortunes. Each of you will *necesitar* to build a little house to *vivir* in, but do not build them of straw *o palos*; straws are brittle and *palos* are frail.

Build your houses of bricks, then you will always have a *seguro sitio* to *vivir* in; you can *ir* in and lock the door, and nothing can *dañar* you."

Then she said goodbye to the little pigs, and away they went, out into the *mundo*, to make their fortunes.

The Three Little Pigs

The first little pig had not gone *lejos* when he *encontró* an *hombre* with a *carga* of straw. The straw looked so warm, and smelled so good that the little pig *completamente olvidó* what his mother had *dicho* him.

"*Por favor*, sir," said the little pig, "give me *suficiente* straw to build a house to keep me warm through the *largo invierno*."

The *hombre* gave the little pig all the straw he wanted, and then he drove away.

C.5.02

The little pig built himself a house of straw, and it was so warm and cosy that he was *encantado* with it.

"How *mucho* better," he said "than a house of cold hard bricks."

So he lay there snug and warm, but one day the big bad wolf knocked on the door.

"Little Pig, little pig, let me in!" he cried.

"Not by the hair on my chinny-chin-chin," answered the pig.

"Then I'll *soplar*, and I'll *resoplar*, and I'll blow your house down.'

The little pig *rio* out loud, for he felt very *seguro* in his snug straw house.

"Well, then *sopla*, and then *resopla*, and blow my house down!" he cried.

Well, the wolf did *soplar* and *resoplar*, and he did blow the house down; because it was *solamente* made of straw, and then he ate the pig up.

The second little pig left the forest and ran and ran, until after a time he *encontró* an *hombre* with a big load of *palos*.

The Three Little Pigs

"Oh, kind sir, *por favor* give me some *palos* to build me a little house for the winter time," cried the little pig.

The *hombre* was happy to do this. He gave the pig all the *palos* he wanted, and then he went on his way.

C.5.03

The pig built himself a house of *palos* and it was stronger than the straw house had been.

"How silly my mother was," said the pig, "to tell me to build a brick house. What could be *más* warm and cosy and *seguro* than this?"

And he snuggled down *entre* the *ramas* and leaves and was very happy.

A little time later along came the big bad wolf, and he stopped and knocked on the door.

"Little pig, little pig, let me in!" he cried.

"Not by the hair of my chinny-chin-chin!"

"Then I'll *soplar*, and I'll *resoplar*, and I'll blow your house down."

The little pig *rio* when he heard that, for the walls were thick, and he felt secure.

"Well, then *sopla*, and then *resopla*, and blow my house down."

So the wolf *sopló*, and he *resopló*, and he did blow the house down, and he ate up the little pig that was inside.

Now the third little pig was the smallest pig of all, but he was a very wise little pig, and he *decidió* to do *exactamente* what his mother had *dicho* him to do.

The Three Little Pigs

C.5.04

After he left the forest, he *encontró* the *hombre* driving the wagon full of straw, but he did not *preguntar* for *algo* of it.

Then he *encontró* the *hombre* with the load of *palos*, but he did not *preguntar* for *algo* of them.

Finally, he *encontró* an *hombre* with a load of bricks, and *solamente* then did he stop. He *preguntó* so nicely for *suficiente* bricks to build himself a little house that the *hombre* could not refuse him.

The pig took the bricks and built himself a little house with them. It took a lot of time and a lot of *trabajo*, but finally the house was *terminada*.

When it was done it was not as soft as the little straw house, and it was not as *tibia* as the little *palo* house, but it was a very *segura* strong little house.

After a time the wolf came along and knocked on the door – knock-knock!

"Little pig, little pig, let me in," he called.

"Not by the hair on my chinny-chin-chin."

"Then I'll *soplar*, and I'll *resoplar*, and I'll blow your house down."

"Well, then *sopla*, and then *resopla*, and blow my house down," answered the pig.

C.5.05

So the wolf *sopló* and he *resopló*, and he *resopló* and he *sopló*, and he *SOPLÓ* AND HE *RESOPLÓ* till he *casi* split his sides, but he couldn't blow the house down.

The Three Little Pigs

And the little pig *rio* to himself as he sat *seguro* and comfortable inside his house.

The wolf *vio* there was nothing to gain by blowing, so he sat down and thought and thought.

Then he said, "Little pig, I know where there is a *campo* of fine turnips."

"Where?" *preguntó* the little pig.

"Open the door and I will tell you."

No, the little pig could hear *bastante* well with the door closed.

"It is just up the road three *campos* away," said the wolf, "and if you would like to have some, I will come for you at six o'clock tomorrow morning, and *nosotros* will *ir* and dig them up *juntos*."

"At six o'clock!" said the little pig. "Very good."

Then the wolf *trotó* off home, licking his lips. He was very happy, because he was looking forward to having bacon for breakfast the *próximo* day.

But the *próximo* morning the little pig was up and *listo* by five o'clock.

C.5.06

Off he *trotó* to the turnip *campo* and gathered an *entero bolsa* full of turnips and was home again before the wolf arrived.

At six o'clock the wolf knocked on the door.

"Are you *listo* to *ir* for the turnips, little pig?" he cried.

"*Listo!*" answered the pig. "Why, I was up and off to the *campo* an *hora* ago and I have all the turnips I want, and I'm boiling them for

The Three Little Pigs

breakfast."

"Is that what you did?" said the wolf. And then he thought for a bit.

"Little pig, do you like ripe juicy apples?" he *preguntó*.

Sí, the pig was very fond of apples.

"Then I can tell you where to *encontrar* some."

"Where is that?"

"Over beyond the *colina* in the squire's orchard, and if you don't play *algún truco* I will come for you at five o'clock tomorrow, and *nosotros* will *ir juntos*, and gather some."

Very well; the pig said he would be *listo*.

So, the wolf *trotó* off home, and this time he was very *seguro* that he would have a nice fat little pig for breakfast the *próximo* morning.

C.5.07

The little pig got up at four o'clock the *próximo* day, and off he went to the orchard as fast as his four little feet would *llevar* him.

But the way was *largo*, and the tree was hard to *trepar*, and while he was still up *entre* the *ramas* gathering apples the big bad wolf came loping into the orchard.

The little pig was very *aterrado*, but he kept very *calma* and hoped, up *entre* the leaves, the wolf would not see him.

The wolf peered around, first up one tree and then up another, and finally he spotted the pig up *entre* the *ramas*.

"Why didn't you wait for me?"

"Oh, I knew you would be along soon."

The Three Little Pigs

"How soon are you coming down?"

"When I have picked a few *más* apples."

The wolf sat down at the foot of the tree, and the pig sat up *entre* the *ramas* crunching apples and licking his lips.

"Are they good?" *preguntó* the wolf looking up; his mouth watering.

Sí, they were very good.

"*Por favor* could you throw one down to me?"

Sí, the little pig could do that.

C.5.08

He picked the biggest, reddest apple he could, and then he threw it, but he threw it as *lejos* as he could, and in such a way that it went bouncing and rolling down the slope of the *colina*.

The wolf bounded down the *colina* after it, and while he was catching it, the little pig *trepó* down the tree and ran safely home with his basketful of apples.

When the wolf *encontró* the pig had tricked him again, he was very *enfadado*. He was *más* determined than ever that he would catch the little pig.

He *trotó* off to the little house and knocked on the door.

"Did you get all the apples you wanted?" *preguntó* the wolf.

Sí, the little pig had all he wanted, and he *agradeció* the wolf for telling him about the orchard.

"*Escucha*, little pig, there will be a fine fair over in the town tomorrow," said the wolf.

"Would you like to go?"

The Three Little Pigs

Sí, the little pig would very *mucho* like to go.

"Very well," said the wolf. "Then I will come for you at half-past three tomorrow, and *nosotros* will *ir* juntos."

C.5.09

"Very well," said the little pig. But *largo* before half-past three the *próximo* day, little pig went off to the fair, and he took four bright silver *monedas* with him, because he wanted to *comprar* himself a *mantequilla* churn.

It did not take him *largo* to *comprar* the churn, and then he *empezó* home again, *llevando* it on his back.

But the wolf had *aprendido* a thing *o dos* about the little pig's tricks.

He, too, *empezó* off to the fair *largo* before half-past three, and so it was that the little pig was *solamente* half way home, and had just reached the *cima* of a high *colina*, when he *vio* the wolf come loping up the *colina* directly *hacia* him.

The little pig was *aterrorizado*. He looked all around but he couldn't see *algún sitio* to *esconder*. He decided the best thing he could do was to get inside the churn.

So he *puso* it down and *trepó* inside it. But the *colina* was very steep, and no sooner was the pig inside the churn than it *empezó* to roll down the *colina* slope - bump, bump, bump - over rocks and stones, leaping and bouncing like something *vivo*.

C.5.10

The little pig did not know what was *sucediendo* to him. He *empezó* to squeal at the *cima* of his voice.

The wolf was half-way up the *colina* when he heard the noise. He

The Three Little Pigs

looked up, and there was a great round thing coming bouncing over the rocks *directo* at him, squeaking and squealing as it came.

He gave one look and his hair bristled with fear, and with an *aullido* he *giró* round and ran home as fast as he could.

He didn't stop till he was safe inside his house, and had *cerrado* and locked the door *detrás* him.

There he crouched, trembling and wondering what would *suceder*.

But nothing *sucedió*, and everything was quiet, so after a time the wolf went out and ran over to the pig's house.

"Little pig, little pig! Are you in there?"

Sí, the little pig was sitting by the fire roasting apples.

"Then, *escucha* while I tell you what *sucedió* to me on the way to the fair."

Then the wolf *puso* his nose close to the *grieta* of the door, and *dijo* the little pig all about the great round squealing thing that had chased him down the *colina*.

C.5.11

The little pig *rio* and *rio*.

"I can tell you *exactamente* what the great squealing thing was; it was a churn which I bought at the fair, and I was inside it."

When the wolf heard this, he was so *enfadado* that he decided to have the little pig, even if he had to *trepar* up on the *techo* and *ir* down the chimney to get him.

He stuck his sharp claws in between the bricks of the house and *trepó* right up the side of it and onto the *techo*.

Then he *trepó* up on to the chimney and slid down it, into the fireplace.

But the little pig had heard what he was doing, and was *listo* for him.

He had a big *olla* of boiling water on the fire, and when he heard the wolf slipping and scrabbling down the chimney, he took the *tapa* off the *olla*, and plop... the wolf fell right into the boiling water.

Then the little pig *puso* the *tapa* tight down onto the *olla*, and that was the end of the big bad wolf.

The little pig *vivió* on in *paz* and *abundancia* forever after, and if *algún* other wolf ever came along to bother him, I never heard about it.

The Three Little Pigs

C.6.01

A mother pig and her three little pigs lived *juntos* happily in a wood all through a *largo* summer. But as autumn approached the mother pig called her little ones to her and said;

"Little pigs, the time has come for you to go out into the *mundo* and seek your *propias* fortunes. Each of you will need to build a little house to live in, but do not build them of straw *o* sticks; straws are brittle and sticks are frail.

Build your houses of bricks, then you will always have a safe *sitio* to live in; you can go in and lock the door, and nothing can *dañar* you."

Then she said goodbye to the little pigs, and away they went, out into the *mundo*, to make their fortunes.

The Three Little Pigs

The first little pig had not gone *lejos* when he *encontró* a man with a load of straw. The straw looked so warm, and smelled so good that the little pig completely forgot what his mother had told him.

"*Por favor*, sir," said the little pig, "give me *suficiente* straw to build a house to keep me warm through the *largo* winter."

The man gave the little pig all the straw he wanted, and then he drove away.

C.6.02

The little pig built himself a house of straw, and it was so warm and cosy that he was delighted with it.

"How *mucho* better," he said "than a house of cold hard bricks."

So he lay there snug and warm, but one day the big bad wolf knocked on the door.

"Little pig, little pig, let me in!" he cried.

"Not by the hair on my chinny-chin-chin," answered the pig.

"Then I'll huff, and I'll puff, and I'll blow your house down."

The little pig laughed out loud, for he felt very safe in his snug straw house.

"Well, then huff, and then puff, and blow my house down!" he cried.

Well, the wolf did huff and puff, and he did blow the house down; because it was only made of straw, and then he ate the pig up.

The second little pig left the forest and ran and ran, until after a time he *encontró* a man with a big load of sticks.

"Oh, kind sir, please give me some sticks to build me a little house for the winter time," cried the little pig.

The Three Little Pigs

The man was happy to do this. He gave the pig all the sticks he wanted, and then he went on his way.

C.6.03

The pig built himself a house of sticks and it was stronger than the straw house had been.

"How silly my mother was," said the pig, "to tell me to build a brick house. What could be more warm and cosy and safe than this?"

And he snuggled down among the branches and leaves and was very happy.

A little time later along came the big bad wolf, and he stopped and knocked on the door.

"Little pig, little pig, let me in!" he cried.

"Not by the hair of my chinny-chin-chin!"

"Then I'll huff, and I'll puff, and I'll blow your house down."

The little pig laughed when he heard that, for the walls were thick, and he felt secure.

"Well, then huff, and then puff, and blow my house down."

So the wolf huffed, and he puffed, and he did blow the house down, and he ate up the little pig that was inside.

Now the third little pig was the smallest pig of all, but he was a very wise little pig, and he decided to do exactly what his mother had told him to do.

C.6.04

After he left the forest, he *encontró* the man driving the wagon full

The Three Little Pigs

of straw, but he did not ask for *algo* of it.

Then he *encontró* the man with the load of sticks, but he did not ask for *algo* of them.

Finally, he *encontró* a man with a load of bricks, and only then did he stop. He asked so nicely for *suficiente* bricks to build himself a little house that the man could not refuse him.

The pig took the bricks and built himself a little house with them. It took a lot of time and a lot of work, but finally the house was finished.

When it was done it was not as soft as the little straw house, and it was not as *tibia* as the little stick house, but it was a very safe strong little house.

After a time the wolf came along and knocked on the door – knock-knock!

"Little pig, little pig, let me in," he called.

"Not by the hair on my chinny-chin-chin."

"Then I'll huff, and I'll puff, and I'll blow your house down."

"Well, then huff, and then puff, and blow my house down," answered the pig.

C.6.05

So the wolf huffed and he puffed, and he puffed and he huffed, and he HUFFED AND HE PUFFED till he almost split his sides, but he couldn't blow the house down.

And the little pig laughed to himself as he sat safe and comfortable inside his house.

The wolf saw there was nothing to gain by blowing, so he sat down and thought and thought.

The Three Little Pigs

Then he said, "Little pig, I know where there is a field of fine turnips."

"Where?" asked the little pig.

"Open the door and I will tell you."

No, the little pig could hear *bastante* well with the door closed.

"It is just up the road three fields away," said the wolf, "and if you would like to have some, I will come for you at six o'clock tomorrow morning, and we will go and dig them up together."

"At six o'clock!" said the little pig. "Very good."

Then the wolf *trotó* off home, licking his lips. He was very happy, because he was looking forward to having bacon for breakfast the *próximo* day.

But the *próximo* morning the little pig was up and *listo* by five o'clock.

C.6.06

Off he *trotó* to the turnip field and gathered a whole *bolsa* full of turnips and was home again before the wolf arrived.

At six o'clock the wolf knocked on the door.

"Are you *listo* to go for the turnips, little pig?" he cried.

"*Listo!*" answered the pig. "Why, I was up and off to the field an hour ago and I have all the turnips I want, and I'm boiling them for breakfast."

"Is that what you did?" said the wolf. And then he thought for a bit.

"Little pig, do you like ripe juicy apples?" he asked.

Yes, the pig was very fond of apples.

The Three Little Pigs

"Then I can tell you where to *encontrar* some."

"Where is that?"

"Over beyond the hill in the squire's orchard, and if you don't play *algún* tricks I will come for you at five o'clock tomorrow, and we will go together, and gather some."

Very well; the pig said he would be *listo*.

So, the wolf *trotó* off home, and this time he was very sure that he would have a nice fat little pig for breakfast the *próximo* morning.

C.6.07

The little pig got up at four o'clock the *próximo* day, and off he went to the orchard as fast as his four little feet would carry him.

But the way was *largo*, and the tree was hard to climb, and while he was still up among the branches gathering apples the big bad wolf came loping into the orchard.

The little pig was very frightened, but he kept very *calma* and hoped, up among the leaves, the wolf would not see him.

The wolf peered around, first up one tree and then up another, and finally he spotted the pig up among the branches.

"Why didn't you wait for me?"

"Oh, I knew you would be along soon."

"How soon are you coming down?"

"When I have picked a few more apples."

The wolf sat down at the foot of the tree, and the pig sat up among the branches crunching apples and licking his lips.

"Are they good?" asked the wolf looking up; his mouth watering.

The Three Little Pigs

Yes, they were very good.

"Please could you throw one down to me?"

Yes, the little pig could do that.

C.6.08

He picked the biggest, reddest apple he could, and then he threw it, but he threw it as *lejos* as he could, and in such a way that it went bouncing and rolling down the slope of the hill.

The wolf bounded down the hill after it, and while he was catching it, the little pig climbed down the tree and ran safely home with his basketful of apples.

When the wolf *encontró* the pig had tricked him again, he was very *enfadó*. He was more determined than ever that he would catch the little pig.

He *trotó* off to the little house and knocked on the door.

"Did you get all the apples you wanted?" asked the wolf.

Yes, the little pig had all he wanted, and he thanked the wolf for telling him about the orchard.

"Listen, little pig, there will be a fine fair over in the town tomorrow," said the wolf.

"Would you like to go?"

Yes, the little pig would very mucho like to go.

"Very well," said the wolf. "Then I will come for you at half-past three tomorrow, and we will go together."

The Three Little Pigs

C.6.09

"Very well," said the little pig. But *largo* before half-past three the *próximo* day, little pig went off to the fair, and he took four bright silver coins with him, because he wanted to buy himself a *mantequilla* churn.

It did not take him *largo* to buy the churn, and then he *empezó* home again, carrying it on his back.

But the wolf had learned a thing *o* two about the little pig's tricks.

He, too, *empezó* off to the fair *largo* before half-past three, and so it was that the little pig was only half way home, and had just reached the top of a high hill, when he saw the wolf come loping up the hill directly *hacia* him.

The little pig was terrified. He looked all around but he couldn't see *algún sitio* to hide. He decided the best thing he could do was to get inside the churn.

So he *puso* it down and *trepó* inside it. But the hill was very steep, and no sooner was the pig inside the churn than it *empezó* to roll down the hill slope - bump, bump, bump - over rocks and stones, leaping and bouncing like something alive.

C.6.10

The little pig did not know what was happening to him. He *empezó* to squeal at the top of his voice.

The wolf was half-way up the hill when he heard the noise. He looked up, and there was a great round thing coming bouncing over the rocks *directo* at him, squeaking and squealing as it came.

He gave one look and his hair bristled with fear, and with a howl he *giró* round and ran home as fast as he could.

The Three Little Pigs

He didn't stop till he was safe inside his house, and had shut and locked the door behind him.

There he crouched, trembling and wondering what would happen.

But nothing happened, and everything was quiet, so after a time the wolf went out and ran over to the pig's house.

"Little pig, little pig! Are you in there?"

Yes, the little pig was sitting by the fire roasting apples.

"Then, listen while I tell you what happened to me on the way to the fair."

Then the wolf *puso* his nose close to the crack of the door, and told the little pig all about the great round squealing thing that had chased him down the hill.

C.6.11

The little pig laughed and laughed.

"I can tell you exactly what the great squealing thing was; it was a churn which I bought at the fair, and I was inside it."

When the wolf heard this, he was so *enfadado* that he decided to have the little pig, even if he had to climb up on the *techo* and go down the chimney to get him.

He stuck his sharp claws in between the bricks of the house and climbed right up the side of it and onto the *techo*.

Then he climbed up on to the chimney and slid down it, into the fireplace.

But the little pig had heard what he was doing, and was *listo* for him.

He had a big pot of boiling water on the fire, and when he heard the wolf slipping and scrabbling down the chimney, he took the lid off the pot, and plop... the wolf fell right into the boiling water.

Then the little pig *puso* the lid tight down onto the pot, and that was the end of the big bad wolf.

The little pig lived on in peace and plenty forever after, and if *algún* other wolf ever came along to bother him, I never heard about it.

The Three Little Pigs

C.7.01

A mother pig and her three little pigs lived together happily in a wood all through a long summer. But as autumn approached the mother pig called her little ones to her and said;

"Little pigs, the time has come for you to go out into the world and seek your own fortunes. Each of you will need to build a little house to live in, but do not build them of straw or sticks; straws are brittle and sticks are frail.

Build your houses of bricks, then you will always have a safe place to live in; you can go in and lock the door, and nothing can harm you."

Then she said goodbye to the little pigs, and away they went, out into the world, to make their fortunes.

The first little pig had not gone far when he met a man with a load of straw. The straw looked so warm, and smelled so good that the little pig completely forgot what his mother had told him.

"Please, sir," said the little pig, "give me enough straw to build a house to keep me warm through the long winter."

The man gave the little pig all the straw he wanted, and then he drove away.

C.7.02

The little pig built himself a house of straw, and it was so warm and cosy that he was delighted with it.

"How much better," he said "than a house of cold hard bricks."

So he lay there snug and warm, but one day the big bad wolf knocked on the door.

"Little Pig, little pig, let me in!" he cried.

"Not by the hair on my chinny-chin-chin," answered the pig.

"Then I'll huff, and I'll puff, and I'll blow your house down."

The little pig laughed out loud, for he felt very safe in his snug straw house.

"Well, then huff, and then puff, and blow my house down!" he cried.

Well, the wolf did huff and puff, and he did blow the house down; because it was only made of straw, and then he ate the pig up.

The second little pig left the forest and ran and ran, until after a time he met a man with a big load of sticks.

"Oh, kind sir, please give me some sticks to build me a little house for the winter time," cried the little pig.

The man was happy to do this. He gave the pig all the sticks he wanted, and then he went on his way.

The Three Little Pigs

C.7.03

The pig built himself a house of sticks and it was stronger than the straw house had been.

"How silly my mother was," said the pig, "to tell me to build a brick house. What could be more warm and cosy and safe than this?"

And he snuggled down among the branches and leaves and was very happy.

A little time later along came the big bad wolf, and he stopped and knocked on the door.

"Little pig, little pig, let me in!" he cried.

"Not by the hair of my chinny-chin-chin!"

"Then I'll huff, and I'll puff, and I'll blow your house down."

The little pig laughed when he heard that, for the walls were thick, and he felt secure.

"Well, then huff, and then puff, and blow my house down."

So the wolf huffed, and he puffed, and he did blow the house down, and he ate up the little pig that was inside.

Now the third little pig was the smallest pig of all, but he was a very wise little pig, and he decided to do exactly what his mother had told him to do.

C.7.04

After he left the forest, he met the man driving the wagon full of straw, but he did not ask for any of it.

Then he met the man with the load of sticks, but he did not ask for any of them.

The Three Little Pigs

Finally, he met a man with a load of bricks, and only then did he stop. He asked so nicely for enough bricks to build himself a little house that the man could not refuse him.

The pig took the bricks and built himself a little house with them. It took a lot of time and a lot of work, but finally the house was finished.

When it was done it was not as soft as the little straw house, and it was not as warm as the little stick house, but it was a very safe strong little house.

After a time the wolf came along and knocked on the door – knock-knock!

"Little pig, little pig, let me in," he called.

"Not by the hair on my chinny-chin-chin."

"Then I'll huff, and I'll puff, and I'll blow your house down."

"Well, then huff, and then puff, and blow my house down," answered the pig.

C.7.05

So the wolf huffed and he puffed, and he puffed and he huffed, and he HUFFED AND HE PUFFED till he almost split his sides, but he couldn't blow the house down.

And the little pig laughed to himself as he sat safe and comfortable inside his house.

The wolf saw there was nothing to gain by blowing, so he sat down and thought and thought.

Then he said, "Little pig, I know where there is a field of fine turnips."

"Where?" asked the little pig.

The Three Little Pigs

"Open the door and I will tell you."

No, the little pig could hear quite well with the door closed.

"It is just up the way three fields away," said the wolf, "and if you would like to have some, I will come for you at six o'clock tomorrow morning, and we will go and dig them up together."

"At six o'clock!" said the little pig. "Very good."

Then the wolf trotted off home, licking his lips. He was very happy, because he was looking forward to having bacon for breakfast the next day.

But the next morning the little pig was up and ready by five o'clock.

C.7.06

Off he trotted to the turnip field and gathered a whole bag full of turnips and was home again before the wolf arrived.

At six o'clock the wolf knocked on the door.

"Are you ready to go for the turnips, little pig?" he cried.

"Ready!" answered the pig. "Why, I was up and off to the field an hour ago and I have all the turnips I want, and I'm boiling them for breakfast."

"Is that what you did?" said the wolf. And then he thought for a bit.

"Little pig, do you like ripe juicy apples?" he asked.

Yes, the pig was very fond of apples.

"Then I can tell you where to find some."

"Where is that?"

"Over beyond the hill in the squire's orchard, and if you don't play

The Three Little Pigs

any tricks I will come for you at five o'clock tomorrow, and we will go together, and gather some."

Very well; the pig said he would be ready.

So, the wolf trotted off home, and this time he was very sure that he would have a nice fat little pig for breakfast the next morning.

C.7.07

The little pig got up at four o'clock the next day, and off he went to the orchard as fast as his four little feet would carry him.

But the way was long, and the tree was hard to climb, and while he was still up among the branches gathering apples the big bad wolf came loping into the orchard.

The little pig was very frightened, but he kept very calm and hoped, up among the leaves, the wolf would not see him.

The wolf peered around, first up one tree and then up another, and finally he spotted the pig up among the branches.

"Why didn't you wait for me?"

"Oh, I knew you would be along soon."

"How soon are you coming down?"

"When I have picked a few more apples."

The wolf sat down at the foot of the tree, and the pig sat up among the branches crunching apples and licking his lips.

"Are they good?" asked the wolf looking up; his mouth watering.

Yes, they were very good.

"Please could you throw one down to me?"

The Three Little Pigs

Yes, the little pig could do that.

C.7.08

He picked the biggest, reddest apple he could, and then he threw it, but he threw it as far as he could, and in such a way that it went bouncing and rolling down the slope of the hill.

The wolf bounded down the hill after it, and while he was catching it, the little pig climbed down the tree and ran safely home with his basketful of apples.

When the wolf found the pig had tricked him again, he was very angry. He was more determined than ever that he would catch the little pig.

He trotted off to the little house and knocked on the door.

"Did you get all the apples you wanted?" asked the wolf.

Yes, the little pig had all he wanted, and he thanked the wolf for telling him about the orchard.

"Listen, little pig, there will be a fine fair over in the town tomorrow," said the wolf.

"Would you like to go?"

Yes, the little pig would very much like to go.

"Very well," said the wolf. "Then I will come for you at half-past three tomorrow, and we will go together."

C.7.09

"Very well," said the little pig. But long before half-past three the next day, little pig went off to the fair, and he took four bright silver coins with him, because he wanted to buy himself a butter churn.

It did not take him long to buy the churn, and then he started home again, carrying it on his back.

But the wolf had learned a thing or two about the little pig's tricks.

He, too, started off to the fair long before half-past three, and so it was that the little pig was only half way home, and had just reached the top of a high hill, when he saw the wolf come loping up the hill directly toward him.

The little pig was terrified. He looked all around but he couldn't see any place to hide. He decided the best thing he could do was to get inside the churn.

So he put it down and crept inside it. But the hill was very steep, and no sooner was the pig inside the churn than it began to roll down the hill slope - bump, bump, bump - over rocks and stones, leaping and bouncing like something alive.

C.7.10

The little pig did not know what was happening to him. He began to squeal at the top of his voice.

The wolf was half-way up the hill when he heard the noise. He looked up, and there was a great round thing coming bouncing over the rocks directo at him, squeaking and squealing as it came.

He gave one look and his hair bristled with fear, and with a howl he turned round and ran home as fast as he could.

He didn't stop till he was safe inside his house, and had shut and locked the door behind him.

There he crouched, trembling and wondering what would happen.

But nothing happened, and everything was quiet, so after a while

The Three Little Pigs

the wolf went out and ran over to the pig's house.

"Little pig, little pig! Are you in there?"

Yes, the little pig was sitting by the fire roasting apples.

"Then, listen while I tell you what happened to me on the way to the fair."

Then the wolf put his nose close to the crack of the door, and told the little pig all about the great round squealing thing that had chased him down the hill.

C.7.11

The little pig laughed and laughed.

"I can tell you exactly what the great squealing thing was; it was a churn which I bought at the fair, and I was inside it."

When the wolf heard this, he was so angry that he decided to have the little pig, even if he had to climb up on the roof and go down the chimney to get him.

He stuck his sharp claws in between the bricks of the house and climbed right up the side of it and onto the roof.

Then he climbed up on to the chimney and slid down it, into the fireplace.

But the little pig had heard what he was doing, and was ready for him.

He had a big pot of boiling water on the fire, and when he heard the wolf slipping and scrabbling down the chimney, he took the lid off the pot, and plop… the wolf fell right into the boiling water.

Then the little pig put the lid tight down onto the pot, and that was the end of the big bad wolf.

The Three Little Pigs

The little pig lived on in peace and plenty forever after, and if any other wolf ever came along to bother him, I never heard about it.

D
Notas finales

Una vez que hayas leído el nivel C.7 y lo hayas entendido de manera general, debes pasar al libro 3, *Little Red Riding-Hood*.

No es necesario que estudies el nivel C.7 de *The Three Little Pigs* en detalle en este momento.

La siguiente sección es Un poco de gramática. Este apartado no es imprescindible. Si no te gusta estudiar gramática, ignora la sección E y continúa con el libro 3.

E
Un poco de gramática – Verbos estándar

E.1 Verbos

Los verbos en inglés son más fáciles que los verbos en castellano en muchos sentidos.

En la mayoría de los casos, el inglés utiliza una raíz verbal simple combinada con auxiliares para formar diferentes tiempos.

El inglés sólo cambia la raíz del verbo por el pasado simple, participio continuo y participio pasado, y también por la tercera persona del singular del presente.

Una gran excepción a esta simplicidad son algunos de los verbos auxiliares como «hacer» y los verbos compuestos. Los verbos auxiliares se analizan en la sección E del libro 3, los verbos compuestos se analizan en la sección E del libro 4.

E.1.1 Raíz verbal

En muchas construcciones verbales en inglés sólo se utiliza la raíz del verbo; es decir, la forma base sin añadir terminaciones o conjugaciones adicionales. Esta forma base del verbo es independiente y no requiere de auxiliares o modificadores:

drink, throw, walk, want, etc.

Normalmente este no es el caso en castellano.

En castellano la raíz verbal generalmente sólo existe en imperativo y en tercera persona del singular presente simple.

drink! – ¡bebe!

Victoria drinks / is drinking – Victoria bebe.

E.1.2 Infinitivo

Uno de los usos más comunes de la raíz verbal en inglés es traducir el infinitivo castellano:

to drink – beber;

to walk – andar.

Aquí «*to*» no significa «a» en castellano, es simplemente una palabra gramatical equivalente al sufijo «-ar / -er / -ir».

Victoria wants to drink some water – Victoria quiere beber agua;

David had to throw the ball – David tuvo que tirar la pelota;

Victoria needed to go – Victoria necesitaba irse.

Es importante tener en cuenta que en inglés el infinitivo se puede dividir, lo que puede dificultar su localización:

Victoria asked him to quietly wait in the house – Victoria le pidió que esperara tranquilamente en la casa.

Aquí el infinitivo «to wait» ha sido dividido por el adverbio «tranquilamente».

Entonces, a veces, si en inglés ves la palabra «*to*» y obviamente no tiene el significado direccional de «a» o «hacia» en castellano, entonces debes buscar un verbo en algún lugar después de «*to*».

E.2 Tiempos presentes

E.2.1 Participio continuo

Los verbos continuos inglés son muy parecidos a los del castellano. El inglés usa el sufijo «*-ing*» mientras que el castellano usa «-ando» o «-(i)endo».

La forma continua se utiliza para mostrar que una acción está en curso.

drinking – bebiendo;

throwing – lanzando.

Como en castellano, el participio continuo se puede utilizar como sustantivo, véase E.2.4 a continuación.

El inglés usa el tiempo continuo en los mismos lugares que en el castellano, usando el verbo «*to be*» donde el castellano usa «estar».

Victoria is drinking – Victoria está bebiendo / Victoria bebe.

Pero el inglés usa el continuo de manera mucho más generalizada y normalmente usa el continuo mientras que otros idiomas usan el tiempo presente simple:

Victoria is studying her science book – Victoria está estudiando su libro de ciencias.

Victoria is studying science – Victoria estudia ciencias.

E.2.2 Presente simple

En inglés sólo los verbos que muestran un estado usan la forma del presente simple. Verbos como «*feel* – sentir», «*want* – querer», «*think* – pensar», «*know* – saber / conocer», «*agree* – estar de acuerdo».

Victoria wants a house – Victoria quiere una casa;

David knows Victoria – David conoce a Victoria;

Victoria agrees with David – Victoria está de acuerdo con David.

Los verbos de acción en inglés, es decir, la mayoría de los verbos, siempre usan la construcción continua para el tiempo presente:

Victoria is working – Victoria trabaja;

David is drinking – David bebe.

E.2.3 Presente habitual

Para los verbos de acción en inglés, la construcción que se parece al presente simple en castellano normalmente es el presente habitual. Lo habitual muestra acontecimientos que suceden de forma regular o repetida.

Lo habitual en inglés se suele expresar utilizando el imperfecto en castellano.

people drink water every day – la gente bebe agua todos los días;

every day you talk to your parents – todos los días, hablas con tus padres.

Sólo con la tercera persona del singular del presente simple / presente habitual, la raíz del verbo tiene una terminación final en «-s». Todas las demás formas toman la raíz simple.

David feels sad – David se siente triste;

every day Victoria talks to her parents – todos los días, Victoria habla con sus padres.

E.2.4 Infinitivos y gerundios

Cuando el participio continuo se utiliza como sustantivo, se llama gerundio.

Tanto el castellano como el inglés pueden utilizar infinitivos y participios presentes como sustantivos.

El inglés suele utilizar gerundios mientras que el castellano utilizaría un infinitivo. A menudo, no es obvio por qué el inglés elige utilizar un infinitivo o un gerundio.

I want to swim – quiero nadar;

I am scared of swimming – tengo miedo de nadar;

swimming is good for your health – nadar es bueno para la salud;

I enjoy swimming – me gusta nadar.

E.3 Tiempos pasados

Los verbos en inglés tienen dos formas de tiempo pasado: el pasado simple y el participio pasado.

E.3.1 Participio pasado

El participio pasado normalmente se usa con el verbo auxiliar «*to have*» de la misma manera que el castellano usa «haber».

El participio pasado en inglés normalmente se forma añadiendo los sufijos «-d» o «-ed» a la raíz del verbo y esto es muy similar en castellano.

Victoria has decided – Victoria ha decidido.

Victoria had decided – Victoria había decidido.

E.3.2 Pasado simple

Para la mayoría de los verbos en inglés, el pasado simple usa la misma forma que el participio pasado:

Victoria decided – Victoria decidió;

we trotted – trotamos.

Aquí el pasado simple en inglés normalmente se traduciría por el pretérito en castellano, pero a menudo el castellano puede usar el imperfecto mientras que el inglés usa el pasado simple.

David studied German – David estudiaba alemán / David estudió alemán.

E.3.3 Formas irregulares del pasado

En la mayoría de los casos, para los verbos regulares el pasado simple y el participio pasado en inglés son idénticos.

Victoria decided – Victoria decidió;

Victoria has decided – Victoria ha decidido;

the pig trotted – el cerdo trotó;

the pig has trotted – el cerdo ha trotado.

Sin embargo, el inglés tiene muchos verbos irregulares en los que el pasado simple y el participio pasado son diferentes. Hay alrededor de doscientos de estos verbos de uso común, y también algunos son de los más utilizados. Desafortunadamente, estos deben aprenderse individualmente. A continuación, se dan algunos ejemplos en la tabla E.3.3.

Tabla E.3.3		
Raíz	*Pasado simple*	*Participio pasado*
bite	bit	bitten
blow	blew	blown
break	broke	broken
drink	drank	drunk
eat	ate	eaten
go	went	gone
hit	hit	hit
swell	swelled	swollen
stand	stood	stood

Ten en cuenta que en el diccionario he traducido formas pasadas en inglés con una sola palabra para el participio pasado. No he incluido todas las formas posibles del pretérito. De modo que en el diccionario tengo:

trotted – trotado;

no:

trotted – trotado, troté, trotaste, trotó, trotamos, trotasteis, trotaron.

Cuando ves un participio pasado del castellano en las secciones del diccionario, esto también implica todas las formas del pretérito.

E.3.4 Pasado habitual

El verbo en inglés «*use*» normalmente es idéntico al del castellano «usar» o «utilizar».

Sin embargo, en inglés el participio pasado «*used*» se convierte en un verbo auxiliar delante de un infinitivo para formar el pasado habitual. Las siguientes oraciones muestran las dos formas diferentes de usar «*use*».

Victoria uses her car to go to work – Victoria usa su coche para ir a trabajar;

Victoria used to cycle to work – Victoria solía ir en bicicleta al trabajo.

Entonces, cuando veas la construcción «*used to*», esto debe traducirse como el tiempo pasado del verbo «soler». De modo que, las dos formas de «*use*» en la siguiente oración tienen significados completamente diferentes.

Victoria used to cycle to work, now she uses her car – Victoria solía ir en bicicleta al trabajo, ahora ella usa su coche.

E.3.5 «To Like»

El verbo «*to like*» en inglés normalmente se traduce como «gustar» en castellano, pero estos dos verbos funcionan de manera diferente.

David likes chocolates – a David le gustan los chocolates.

Esta construcción inglesa funciona exactamente igual en el caso de los verbos «odiar» o «amar» en castellano.

David hates chocolates – David odia los chocolates;

David loves Victoria – David ama a Victoria.

En inglés existe la construcción «*to please*» que es similar a «gustar», pero rara vez se usa.

the house pleases me – la casa me agrada;

F

Palabras - Ordenado por sección

C.1.01	**do**	hago, haces/-emos/-éis/-en - "do" significa 'hacer' o 'fabricar', pero se usa con mayor frecuencia como un verbo auxiliar 'ficticio' en declaraciones negativas o interrogativas. Por ejemplo "they work": 'ellos trabajan , "they don't work": 'ellos no trabajan', "do they work?": '¿trabajan?'. Tenga en cuenta que nunca se usa "to do" para mostrar causalidad en inglés, sino que se usa "make/made". "I make him work": 'Yo lo hago trabajar'.
	him	él, lo, le
	himself	él-mismo
	houses	casas - edeficios
	how	cómo
	them	(a) ellos, ellas
	what	qué

The Three Little Pigs

	will	La forma inglesa "will" es un tiempo futuro que se usa para cosas que están en un futuro más distante, o que son muy probables, pero no casi seguras. Este uso del futuro inglés normalmente se traduce al castellano por el tiempo futuro de indicativo. "he will get that job": 'conseguirá ese trabajo', "if she eats that she will be ill": 'si come, que se enfermará'. La auxiliar "will" también puede indicar deseo, preferencia, consentimiento, elección, capacidad, determinación o insistencia. Comúnmente se contrae "will" a "-'ll". La contracción negativa de "will not" es irregular "won't".
	you	tú, usted, vos, vosotros, ustedes, te, lo, le
	your	tu(s), su(s), vuestro/a(s), suyo/a(s)
C.1.02	I	yo
	stopped	detenido, parado
	stronger	más fuerte
C.1.03	done	hecho
	smallest	lo más pequeño
	strong	fuerte
C.1.04	along	a lo largo de
	doing	haciendo
	end	final, fin
	ever	siempre
	forever	para siempre
	onto	sobre, en
C.2.01	better	mejor
	each	cada
	pig	cerdo
	pigs	cerdos
	seek	busca
	warm	tibio, cálido, calenta
	wolf	lobo
C.2.02	blow	sopla, golpe
	later	mas tarde
C.2.03	couldn't	could not - no podía/-as/-amos/-ais/-an
	knock-knock	toc-toc

The Three Little Pigs

	sides	lados
	till	hasta, hasta que, labra, caja registradora
	wise	sabio
C.2.04	any	algún, algunos
	bother	molesta
	chimney	chimenea - estructura por salida de humos
	claws	garras
	even	incluso
	other	otro
	scrabbling	escarbando
	side	lado
	slipping	resbalando, deslizando
C.3.01	always	siempre
	an	un, uno, una - se usa cuando la siguiente palabra comienza con un sonido de vocal
	are	eres, somos, sois, son, estás, estamos, estáis, están
	can	lata, puedo/-es/-e/-emos/-éis/-en
	gave	dado
	lock	cerradura, cerrar con llave, bucle
	make	fabricar - sin embargo, se usa "make/made" más comúnmente para mostrar causalidad. "I make them work": 'hago que trabajan".
	ones	En este contexto, "one" o "ones" se refiere a personas o cosas conocidas y generalmente se traducirá con 'los'. Este es el mismo "one" que existe en compuestos como "someone": 'alguien', "anyone": 'cualquiera o "everyone": 'todos'. Asi que; "little ones": 'los pequeños', "older ones": 'los mayores". Tenga en cuenta que "ones" no significa 'unos, unas'. Las palabras 'unos' y 'unas' se traducen con la palabra "some".
	wood	madera, bosque
C.3.02	chinny-chin-chin	mentoncito-mentón-mentón

The Three Little Pigs

	I'll		I will - La forma inglesa "will" es un tiempo futuro que se usa para cosas que están en un futuro más distante, o que son muy probables, pero no casi seguras. Este uso del futuro inglés normalmente se traduce al castellano por el tiempo futuro de indicativo. "he will get that job": 'conseguirá ese trabajo', "if she eats that she will be ill": 'si come, que se enfermará'. La auxiliar "will" también puede indicar deseo, preferencia, consentimiento, elección, capacidad, determinación o insistencia. Comúnmente se contrae "will" a "-'ll".
	some		unos, unas, algunos, algunas
	way		forma, manera, camino, dirección
C.3.04	**lot**		mucho, un montón de
	nicely		bien, de buena manera
C.3.05	**fine**		bien, bueno, fino, multa
	forward		hacia adelante - "look forward to": 'anticipar'
	having		teniendo
	hear		escucha
	morning		(por la) mañana - antes de medio día
	o'clock		of the clock - en punto (de hora)
	road		camino, carreterra
	tomorrow		mañana - el día despues de hoy
C.3.06	**ago**		atrás, hace
	beyond		más allá de
	bit		un poco, mordido
	don't		do not - no hago, haces/-emos/-éis/-en - "do" significa 'hacer' o 'fabricar', pero se usa con mayor frecuencia como un verbo auxiliar 'ficticio' en declaraciones negativas o interrogativas. Por ejemplo "they work": 'ellos trabajan', "they don't work": 'ellos no trabajan', "do they work?": '¿trabajan?'. Tenga en cuenta que nunca se usa "to do" para mostrar causalidad en inglés, sino que se usa "make/made". "I make him work": 'Yo lo hago trabajar'.
	fond		gustar, cariñoso - "he is fond of apples": 'le gustan las manzanas', "he is fond of her": 'él es aficionado a ella'.
	gathered		recolectado

The Three Little Pigs

	I'm	I am - estoy, soy
	nice	amable, bonito, lindo
	squire's	squire-[su], squire is/has - del hacendado (posesivo), hacendado es/está/había
	want	quiere
	why	por qué, pues
C.3.07	**another**	un otro
	didn't	did not - no hizo, hice/-iste/-imos/-isteis/-icieron - "did" significa 'hecho' o 'fabricado', pero se usa con mayor frecuencia como un verbo auxiliar 'ficticio' en declaraciones negativas o interrogativas. Por ejemplo "they worked": 'ellos trabajaron', "they didn't work": 'ellos no trabajaron', "did they work?": '¿trabajaron?'. Tenga en cuenta que nunca se usa "to do" para mostrar causalidad en inglés, sino que se usa "make/made". "I made him work": 'Yo le hice trabajar'.
	feet	pies
	foot	pie
	gathering	recolectando
	got	obtenido, tenido, muchos otros - las palabras "get" y "got" se usan ampliamente con muchos significados diferentes. Un ejemplo común es el significado de 'cambiar' o 'convertirse'; "they got rich": 'se hicieron ricos'. Se usa con "have" para mostrar posesión; "they've got a new car": 'tienen un auto nuevo'. También se usa "got/get" en muchos verbos frasales; "to get up": 'levantarse', "to get on": 'subirse a'.
	peered	mirado detenidamente
	tree	árbol
	wait	espera
C.3.08	**basketful**	una cesta llena (de)
	biggest	lo más grande
	half-past	y media (de hora) - 'half past four': 'cuatro y media'
	reddest	lo más roja
	such	tan, tanto, tal, semejante
C.3.09	**best**	lo mejor
	half	medio, mitad

The Three Little Pigs

	leaping	saltando
	pig's	pig-[su], pig is/has - del cerdo (posesivo), cerdo es/está/había
	reached	alcanzado, llegado a
	roll	rueda
	sooner	cuanto antes / más temprano
C.3.10	**everything**	todo, todos
	fire	fuego
	locked	cerrado con llave
	look	mira
	squeal	chilla
	squealing	chillando
	wondering	fascinando, curiosa, preguntandose
C.3.11	**fireplace**	chimenea - sitio donde está el fuego
C.4.01	**approached**	acercado
	autumn	otoño
	away	(hacía) fuera
	brittle	frágil
	frail	frágil, débil
	goodbye	adiós
	sir	señor
	summer	verano
C.4.02	**cosy**	acogedor, intimo
	kind	amable, tipo
	loud	ruidoso, sonido fuerte
C.4.03	**secure**	seguro
	silly	absurdo, tonto
	snuggled	acurrucado
	thick	grueso
	walls	paredes
C.4.04	**wagon**	vagón
C.4.05	**bacon**	tocino
	dig	cava
	gain	gana
	split	separa
	where	donde

The Three Little Pigs

C.4.06	**arrived**	llegado
	fat	gordo, grasa
	juicy	jugoso
	ripe	maduro
C.4.07	**crunching**	crujiendo
	mouth	boca
	spotted	disinado, con manchas
	watering	regando, hacerse agua la boca
C.4.08	**bounded**	brincado, limitado
	determined	determinado
	fair	feria, justo, imparcial, rubio, claro, blanco
	town	pueblo grande o ciucad pequño - urbanizacion con un mercado pero sin una catedral
C.4.09	**bump**	choca, bulto, protuberancia
	directly	directamente
	something	algo, alguna cosa
	steep	empinado
	thing	cosa
C.4.10	**bristled**	erizado
	chased	perseguido
	crouched	agachado
	nothing	nada
	quiet	tranquilo, silencioso
	round	redondo
C.4.11	**between**	entre
	bought	comprado
	slid	resbalado, deslizado
	stuck	metido, clavado, pegado
	tight	apretado
C.5.01	**bricks**	ladrillos
	build	construye
	drove	conducido
	fortunes	fortunas
	happily	felizmente
	keep	guarda, conserva - "keep from": 'prevenir'
	straw	paja

The Three Little Pigs

	straws	pajas
C.5.02	bad	malo
	built	construido
	happy	feliz, contento
	load	carga
	snug	acogedor, intimo
	winter	invierno
C.5.03	brick	ladrillo
	leaves	hojas, sales de
	tell	cuenta, dice a
C.5.04	driving	conduciendo
	refuse	nega, rehusa, basura
C.5.05	closed	cerrado
	five	cinco
	licking	lamiendo
	lips	labios
	six	seis
	turnips	nabos
C.5.06	apples	manzanas
	boiling	hirviendo
	orchard	huerta
	turnip	nabo
C.5.07	few	poco, pocos
	four	cuatro
	kept	guardado, conservado
	loping	dando zancadas
	throw	tira, lanza
C.5.08	apple	manzana
	bouncing	rebotando
	catch	captura
	catching	capturando
	safely	seguramente, sin peligro
	slope	inclinación, cuesta
	telling	diciendo a, contando a
	threw	tirado, lanzado

The Three Little Pigs

	tricked	engañado
C.5.09	churn	lechera, batir
	decided	decidido
	rocks	rocas, piedras
	stones	piedras
	tricks	trucos
C.5.10	close	cerca, cerra
	fear	miedo
	noise	ruido
	nose	nariz
	roasting	asando
	safe	seguro
	trembling	temblando
C.5.11	plop	plaf
	water	agua
C.6.01	completely	completamente
	forgot	olvidado
	go	ir, voy, vas, vamos, vais, van - también se usa "go" para el futuro simple de manera similar a 'ir' en Castellano. se usa "go" para cosas que están en el futuro cercano, ya están planeadas o es casi seguro que sucedan. "Victoria is going to drink": 'Victoria va a beber'
	live	vive, vivo, en vivo
	lived	vivido
	man	hombre
	need	necesita
	sticks	palos
	told	dicho, contado a
C.6.02	delighted	encantado, contento
	huff	sopla, resopla, haz / dar una calada
	laughed	reído
	only	solamente
	please	por favor, complace
	puff	sopla, resopla, haz / dar una calada
C.6.03	among	entre

The Three Little Pigs

	branches	ramas
	exactly	exactamente
	huffed	soplado, resoplado, hecho / dado una calada
	more	más
	puffed	soplado, resoplado, hecho / dado una calada
C.6.04	ask	pregunta
	asked	preguntado
	finished	terminado
	stick	palo
	work	trabajo, trabaja
C.6.05	almost	casi
	field	campo
	fields	campos
	saw	visto
	together	juntos
	we	nosotros
C.6.06	hill	colina
	hour	hora
	sure	seguro
	whole	entero
	yes	sí
C.6.07	carry	lleva - "carry on": 'continuar'
	climb	trepa, sube, ascende
	frightened	aterrado
C.6.08	climbed	trepado, subido, ascendido
	listen	escucha
	thanked	agradecido
C.6.09	alive	vivo, en vivo
	buy	compra
	carrying	llevando
	coins	monedas
	hide	esconde
	learned	aprendido
	terrified	aterrorizado
	top	cima

	two	dos
C.6.10	behind	detrás
	crack	grieta
	happen	sucede
	happened	sucedido
	happening	sucediendo
	howl	aullido
	shut	cerrado
C.6.11	lid	tapa
	peace	paz
	plenty	mucho, suficiente, bastante, abundancia
	pot	olla, maceta
C.7.01	enough	suficiente
	far	lejos
	harm	daño, daña
	long	largo
	met	encontrado
	or	o
	own	propio
	place	sitio
	world	mundo
C.7.02	much	mucho
C.7.05	next	próximo
	quite	bastante
	ready	listo
	trotted	trotado
C.7.06	bag	bolsa
	find	encuentra
C.7.08	angry	enfadado
	found	encontrado
C.7.09	began	empezado
	butter	mantequilla
	crept	trepado
	put	pone, puesto - "put on": 'ponerse'
	started	empezado, sustado

The Three Little Pigs

	toward	hacia (un dirección)
C.7.10	turned	girado, transformado
C.7.11	roof	techo

G
Palabras - Orden Alfabético

ago	atrás, hace	C.3.06
alive	vivo, en vivo	C.6.09
almost	casi	C.6.05
along	a lo largo de	C.1.04
always	siempre	C.3.01
among	entre	C.6.03
an	un, uno, una - se usa cuando la siguiente palabra comienza con un sonido de vocal	C.3.01
angry	enfadado	C.7.08
another	un otro	C.3.07
any	algún, algunos	C.2.04
apple	manzana	C.5.08
apples	manzanas	C.5.06
approached	acercado	C.4.01
are	eres, somos, sois, son, estás, estamos, estáis, están	C.3.01
arrived	llegado	C.4.06
ask	pregunta	C.6.04
asked	preguntado	C.6.04
autumn	otoño	C.4.01
away	(hacía) fuera	C.4.01
bacon	tocino	C.4.05
bad	malo	C.5.02

The Three Little Pigs

bag	bolsa	C.7.06
basketful	una cesta llena (de)	C.3.08
began	empezado	C.7.09
behind	detrás	C.6.10
best	lo mejor	C.3.09
better	mejor	C.2.01
between	entre	C.4.11
beyond	más allá de	C.3.06
biggest	lo más grande	C.3.08
bit	un poco, mordido	C.3.06
blow	sopla, golpe	C.2.02
boiling	hirviendo	C.5.06
bother	molesta	C.2.04
bought	comprado	C.4.11
bouncing	rebotando	C.5.08
bounded	brincado, limitado	C.4.08
branches	ramas	C.6.03
brick	ladrillo	C.5.03
bricks	ladrillos	C.5.01
bristled	erizado	C.4.10
brittle	frágil	C.4.01
build	construye	C.5.01
built	construido	C.5.02
bump	choca, bulto, protuberancia	C.4.09
butter	mantequilla	C.7.09
buy	compra	C.6.09
can	lata, puedo/-es/-e/-emos/-éis/-en	C.3.01
carry	lleva - "carry on": 'continuar'	C.6.07
carrying	llevando	C.6.09
catch	captura	C.5.08
catching	capturando	C.5.08
chased	perseguido	C.4.10
chimney	chimenea - estructura por salida de humos	C.2.04
chinny-chin-chin	mentoncito-mentón-mentón	C.3.02
churn	lechera, batir	C.5.09

The Three Little Pigs

claws	garras	C.2.04
climb	trepa, sube, ascende	C.6.07
climbed	trepado, subido, ascendido	C.6.08
close	cerca, cerra	C.5.10
closed	cerrado	C.5.05
coins	monedas	C.6.09
completely	completamente	C.6.01
cosy	acogedor, intimo	C.4.02
couldn't	could not - no podía/-as/-amos/-ais/-an	C.2.03
crack	grieta	C.6.10
crept	trepado	C.7.09
crouched	agachado	C.4.10
crunching	crujiendo	C.4.07
decided	decidido	C.5.09
delighted	encantado, contento	C.6.02
determined	determinado	C.4.08
didn't	did not - no hizo, hice/-iste/-imos/-isteis/-icieron - "did" significa 'hecho' o 'fabricado', pero se usa con mayor frecuencia como un verbo auxiliar 'ficticio' en declaraciones negativas o interrogativas. Por ejemplo "they worked": 'ellos trabajaron', "they didn't work": 'ellos no trabajaron', "did they work?": '¿trabajaron?'. Tenga en cuenta que nunca se usa "to do" para mostrar causalidad en inglés, sino que se usa "make/made". "I made him work": 'Yo le hice trabajar'.	C.3.07
dig	cava	C.4.05
directly	directamente	C.4.09
do	hago, haces/-emos/-éis/-en - "do" significa 'hacer' o 'fabricar', pero se usa con mayor frecuencia como un verbo auxiliar 'ficticio' en declaraciones negativas o interrogativas. Por ejemplo "they work": 'ellos trabajan', "they don't work": 'ellos no trabajan', "do they work?": '¿trabajan?'. Tenga en cuenta que nunca se usa "to do" para mostrar causalidad en inglés, sino que se usa "make/made". "I make him work": 'Yo lo hago trabajar'.	C.1.01
doing	haciendo	C.1.04

don't	do not - no hago, haces/-emos/-éis/-en - "do" significa 'hacer' o 'fabricar', pero se usa con mayor frecuencia como un verbo auxiliar 'ficticio' en declaraciones negativas o interrogativas. Por ejemplo "they work": 'ellos trabajan', "they don't work": 'ellos no trabajan', "do they work?": '¿trabajan?'. Tenga en cuenta que nunca se usa "to do" para mostrar causalidad en inglés, sino que se usa "make/made". "I make him work": 'Yo lo hago trabajar'.	C.3.06
done	hecho	C.1.03
driving	conduciendo	C.5.04
drove	conducido	C.5.01
each	cada	C.2.01
end	final, fin	C.1.04
enough	suficiente	C.7.01
even	incluso	C.2.04
ever	siempre	C.1.04
everything	todo, todos	C.3.10
exactly	exactamente	C.6.03
fair	feria, justo, imparcial, rubio, claro, blanco	C.4.08
far	lejos	C.7.01
fat	gordo, grasa	C.4.06
fear	miedo	C.5.10
feet	pies	C.3.07
few	poco, pocos	C.5.07
field	campo	C.6.05
fields	campos	C.6.05
find	encuentra	C.7.06
fine	bien, bueno, fino, multa	C.3.05
finished	terminado	C.6.04
fire	fuego	C.3.10
fireplace	chimenea - sitio donde está el fuego	C.3.11
five	cinco	C.5.05
fond	gustar, cariñoso - "he is fond of apples": 'le gustan las manzanas', "he is fond of her": 'él es aficionado a ella'.	C.3.06
foot	pie	C.3.07

The Three Little Pigs

forever	para siempre	C.1.04
forgot	olvidado	C.6.01
fortunes	fortunas	C.5.01
forward	hacia adelante - "look forward to": 'anticipar'	C.3.05
found	encontrado	C.7.08
four	cuatro	C.5.07
frail	frágil, débil	C.4.01
frightened	aterrado	C.6.07
gain	gana	C.4.05
gathered	recolectado	C.3.06
gathering	recolectando	C.3.07
gave	dado	C.3.01
go	ir, voy, vas, vamos, vais, van - también se usa "go" para el futuro simple de manera similar a 'ir' en Castellano. se usa "go" para cosas que están en el futuro cercano, ya están planeadas o es casi seguro que sucedan. "Victoria is going to drink": 'Victoria va a beber'	C.6.01
goodbye	adiós	C.4.01
got	obtenido, tenido, muchos otros - las palabras "get" y "got" se usan ampliamente con muchos significados diferentes. Un ejemplo común es el significado de 'cambiar' o 'convertirse'; "they got rich": 'se hicieron ricos'. Se usa con "have" para mostrar posesión; "they've got a new car": 'tienen un auto nuevo'. También se usa "got/get" en muchos verbos frasales; "to get up": 'levantarse', "to get on": 'subirse a'.	C.3.07
half	medio, mitad	C.3.09
half-past	y media (de hora) - 'half past four': 'cuatro y media'	C.3.08
happen	sucede	C.6.10
happened	sucedido	C.6.10
happening	sucediendo	C.6.10
happily	felizmente	C.5.01
happy	feliz, contento	C.5.02
harm	daño, daña	C.7.01
having	teniendo	C.3.05
hear	escucha	C.3.05

The Three Little Pigs

hide	esconde	C.6.09
hill	colina	C.6.06
him	él, lo, le	C.1.01
himself	él-mismo	C.1.01
hour	hora	C.6.06
houses	casas - edeficios	C.1.01
how	cómo	C.1.01
howl	aullido	C.6.10
huff	sopla, resopla, haz / dar una calada	C.6.02
huffed	soplado, resoplado, hecho / dado una calada	C.6.03
I	yo	C.1.02
I'll	I will - La forma inglesa "will" es un tiempo futuro que se usa para cosas que están en un futuro más distante, o que son muy probables, pero no casi seguras. Este uso del futuro inglés normalmente se traduce al castellano por el tiempo futuro de indicativo. "he will get that job": 'conseguirá ese trabajo', "if she eats that she will be ill": 'si come, que se enfermará'. La auxiliar "will" también puede indicar deseo, preferencia, consentimiento, elección, capacidad, determinación o insistencia. Comúnmente se contrae "will" a "-'ll".	C.3.02
I'm	I am - estoy, soy	C.3.06
juicy	jugoso	C.4.06
keep	guarda, conserva - "keep from": 'prevenir'	C.5.01
kept	guardado, conservado	C.5.07
kind	amable, tipo	C.4.02
knock-knock	toc-toc	C.2.03
later	mas tarde	C.2.02
laughed	reído	C.6.02
leaping	saltando	C.3.09
learned	aprendido	C.6.09
leaves	hojas, sales de	C.5.03
licking	lamiendo	C.5.05
lid	tapa	C.6.11
lips	labios	C.5.05
listen	escucha	C.6.08

The Three Little Pigs

live	vive, vivo, en vivo	C.6.01
lived	vivido	C.6.01
load	carga	C.5.02
lock	cerradura, cerrar con llave, bucle	C.3.01
locked	cerrado con llave	C.3.10
long	largo	C.7.01
look	mira	C.3.10
loping	dando zancadas	C.5.07
lot	mucho, un montón de	C.3.04
loud	ruidoso, sonido fuerte	C.4.02
make	fabricar - sin embargo, se usa "make/made" más comúnmente para mostrar causalidad. "I make them work": 'hago que trabajan'.	C.3.01
man	hombre	C.6.01
met	encontrado	C.7.01
more	más	C.6.03
morning	(por la) mañana - antes de medio día	C.3.05
mouth	boca	C.4.07
much	mucho	C.7.02
need	necesita	C.6.01
next	próximo	C.7.05
nice	amable, bonito, lindo	C.3.06
nicely	bien, de buena manera	C.3.04
noise	ruido	C.5.10
nose	nariz	C.5.10
nothing	nada	C.4.10
o'clock	of the clock - en punto (de hora)	C.3.05
ones	En este contexto, "one" o "ones" se refiere a personas o cosas conocidas y generalmente se traducirá con 'los'. Este es el mismo "one" que existe en compuestos como "someone": 'alguien', "anyone": 'cualquiera' o "everyone": 'todos'. Asi que; "little ones": 'los pequeños', "older ones": 'los mayores". Tenga en cuenta que "ones" no significa 'unos, unas'. Las palabras 'unos' y 'unas' se traducen con la palabra "some".	C.3.01
only	solamente	C.6.02

The Three Little Pigs

onto	sobre, en	**C.1.04**
or	o	**C.7.01**
orchard	huerta	**C.5.06**
other	otro	**C.2.04**
own	propio	**C.7.01**
peace	paz	**C.6.11**
peered	mirado detenidamente	**C.3.07**
pig	cerdo	**C.2.01**
pig's	pig-[su], pig is/has - del cerdo (posesivo), cerdo es/está/había	**C.3.09**
pigs	cerdos	**C.2.01**
place	sitio	**C.7.01**
please	por favor, complace	**C.6.02**
plenty	mucho, suficiente, bastante, abundancia	**C.6.11**
plop	plaf	**C.5.11**
pot	olla, maceta	**C.6.11**
puff	sopla, resopla, haz / dar una calada	**C.6.02**
puffed	soplado, resoplado, hecho / dado una calada	**C.6.03**
put	pone, puesto - "put on": 'ponerse'	**C.7.09**
quiet	tranquilo, silencioso	**C.4.10**
quite	bastante	**C.7.05**
reached	alcanzado, llegado a	**C.3.09**
ready	listo	**C.7.05**
reddest	lo más roja	**C.3.08**
refuse	nega, rehusa, basura	**C.5.04**
ripe	maduro	**C.4.06**
road	camino, carreterra	**C.3.05**
roasting	asando	**C.5.10**
rocks	rocas, piedras	**C.5.09**
roll	rueda	**C.3.09**
roof	techo	**C.7.11**
round	redondo	**C.4.10**
safe	seguro	**C.5.10**
safely	seguramente, sin peligro	**C.5.08**
saw	visto	**C.6.05**
scrabbling	escarbando	**C.2.04**

The Three Little Pigs

secure	seguro	C.4.03
seek	busca	C.2.01
shut	cerrado	C.6.10
side	lado	C.2.04
sides	lados	C.2.03
silly	absurdo, tonto	C.4.03
sir	señor	C.4.01
six	seis	C.5.05
slid	resbalado, deslizado	C.4.11
slipping	resbalando, deslizando	C.2.04
slope	inclinación, cuesta	C.5.08
smallest	lo más pequeño	C.1.03
snug	acogedor, intimo	C.5.02
snuggled	acurrucado	C.4.03
some	unos, unas, algunos, algunas	C.3.02
something	algo, alguna cosa	C.4.09
sooner	cuanto antes / más temprano	C.3.09
split	separa	C.4.05
spotted	disinado, con manchas	C.4.07
squeal	chilla	C.3.10
squealing	chillando	C.3.10
squire's	squire-[su], squire is/has - del hacendado (posesivo), hacendado es/esté/había	C.3.06
started	empezado, sustado	C.7.09
steep	empinado	C.4.09
stick	palo	C.6.04
sticks	palos	C.6.01
stones	piedras	C.5.09
stopped	detenido, parado	C.1.02
straw	paja	C.5.01
straws	pajas	C.5.01
strong	fuerte	C.1.03
stronger	más fuerte	C.1.02
stuck	metido, clavado, pegado	C.4.11
such	tan, tanto, tal, semejante	C.3.08
summer	verano	C.4.01

The Three Little Pigs

sure	seguro	C.6.06
tell	cuenta, dice a	C.5.03
telling	diciendo a, contando a	C.5.08
terrified	aterrorizado	C.6.09
thanked	agradecido	C.6.08
them	(a) ellos, ellas	C.1.01
thick	grueso	C.4.03
thing	cosa	C.4.09
threw	tirado, lanzado	C.5.08
throw	tira, lanza	C.5.07
tight	apretado	C.4.11
till	hasta, hasta que, labra, caja registradora	C.2.03
together	juntos	C.6.05
told	dicho, contado a	C.6.01
tomorrow	mañana - el día despues de hoy	C.3.05
top	cima	C.6.09
toward	hacia (un dirección)	C.7.09
town	pueblo grande o ciudad pequño - urbanizacion con un mercado pero sin una catedral	C.4.08
tree	árbol	C.3.07
trembling	temblando	C.5.10
tricked	engañado	C.5.08
tricks	trucos	C.5.09
trotted	trotado	C.7.05
turned	girado, transformado	C.7.10
turnip	nabo	C.5.06
turnips	nabos	C.5.05
two	dos	C.6.09
wagon	vagón	C.4.04
wait	espera	C.3.07
walls	paredes	C.4.03
want	quiere	C.3.06
warm	tibio, cálido, calenta	C.2.01
water	agua	C.5.11
watering	regando, hacerse agua la boca	C.4.07
way	forma, manera, camino, dirección	C.3.02

The Three Little Pigs

we	nosotros	C.6.05
what	qué	C.1.01
where	donde	C.4.05
whole	entero	C.6.06
why	por qué, pues	C.3.06
will	La forma inglesa "will" es un tiempo futuro que se usa para cosas que están en un futuro más distante, o que son muy probables, pero no casi seguras. Este uso del futuro inglés normalmente se traduce al castellano por el tiempo futuro de indicativo. "he will get that job": 'conseguirá ese trabajo', "if she eats that she will be ill": 'si come, que se enfermará'. La auxiliar "will" también puede indicar deseo, preferencia, consentimiento, elección, capacidad, determinación o insistencia. Comúnmente se contrae "will" a "-'ll".	C.1.01
winter	invierno	C.5.02
wise	sabio	C.2.03
wolf	lobo	C.2.01
wondering	fascinando, curiosa, preguntandose	C.3.10
wood	madera, bosque	C.3.01
work	trabajo, trabaja	C.6.04
world	mundo	C.7.01
yes	sí	C.6.06
you	tú, usted, vos, vosotros, ustedes, te, lo, le	C.1.01
your	tu(s), su(s), vuestro/a(s), suyo/a(s)	C.1.01

www.ingramcontent.com/pod-product-compliance
Lightning Source LLC
Chambersburg PA
CBHW052103070526
44584CB00017B/2316